The Theory of Learners

An Introduction

Julie Cotton

KOGAN
PAGE

London • Philadelphia

To all my learners.

First published in 1995

Apart from any fair dealing for the purposes of research or private study, or criticism or review, as permitted under the Copyright, Designs and Patents Act, 1988, this publication may only be reproduced, stored or transmitted, in any form or by any means, with the prior permission in writing of the publishers, or in the case of reprographic reproduction in accordance with the terms of licences issued by the Copyright Licensing Agency. Enquiries concerning reproduction outside those terms should be sent to the publishers at the undermentioned address:

Kogan Page Limited
120 Pentonville Road
London N1 9JN

© Julie Cotton, 1995

British Library Cataloguing in Publication Data

A CIP record for this book is available from the British Library

ISBN 0 7494 1479 0

Typeset by Saxon Graphics Ltd, Derby
Printed and bound in Great Britain by Biddles Ltd, Guildford and King's Lynn

Theory of
Learners

Also in the Learning and Assessment Theory series

Contents

Introduction

This book is for every full-time and part-time teacher including trainers, further education lecturers, work-based skills trainers, higher education lecturers, adult education lecturers, instructors, professors, open-learning managers, tutors, distance learning writers, counsellors, mentors, staff development managers and even, as one of my students called himself, apprentice masters. We are all concerned with the business of helping individual learners and we may even gain a few tips on how to improve our own learning if we study the theory of learners.

The content of this book concentrates on learners as individual and unique people who have to be treated with respect and who have rights. Book one in the series looked at the things that learners have in common by studying general learning theory; here we look at the individuality of learners. The strategies for helping other people to learn are covered in book three and the theory of assessment and evaluation is the subject for book four.

After 25 years of training for vocational, technical, higher and adult education I have never come across a book which covers the topic of the adolescent and adult learner in a user-friendly way. I have had to scour a few general books on social psychology, some on philosophy and collect a large number of diverse sources to put together this book. Good and helpful books have been written in related fields – such as counselling and child development – but study of the older learner in the current educational and training climate seems to be sadly neglected.

In this introductory book I have tried to assume that the reader has nothing but an interest in individual learners but it is very difficult to avoid the jargon which bedevils any writing about education and training. I have included a few suggestions for activities which may help you to apply theory to your own work. Without offence to the reader, I hope, I have suggested places where you might stop and have a good think about what the theory means in practice. To this end I have asked some open questions which are intended to trigger your thoughts rather than come to any hard and fast conclusions. You may find the chapters readable in their own right but I have placed the main concepts at the beginning of each chapter in case you want to use the book as a traditional reference.

Remember that this is only an introduction to the theory of learners and maybe your pet theory is missing! After the first four books in the series I intend to revisit each of the four topics in turn but at a more advanced level of study so that the second phase of the series will be pitched at graduate level. Some books call themselves an 'Introduction' and they are, in reality, fiendishly complicated, so I hope that I have not indulged in such one-up-manship and you find this book a helpful introduction to the topic of learners.

Chapter 1

Individual Differences, Self-image and Self-esteem

EACH PERSON IS UNIQUE

Most learning theories are all right for other people but I would not like them to be applied to me. I am more than a series of chemical reactions in a set of muscles and nerves which is how a physiologist would regard me. Like me, I do not expect that you would like to be seen as a frantic ego trying to balance the id and the superego, but that is how a Freudian psychologist would see you. The behaviourists are not much better because in stimulus-response psychology you and I are little more than mindless puppets to be manipulated by those in authority. All these approaches to learning were covered in the first book of the series. In this book we are going to look at the learner as an individual. At times you may be confused because I may be talking about you and not your students or trainees. This is quite deliberate because knowing yourself is one of the best ways of helping you to treat each learner as an individual person.

Personality is a total picture of an individual. It is important that we make a realistic assessment of our own strengths and weaknesses so that we can concentrate on effective living rather than wallow in self-deception. The teacher or the trainer must remember that all learners are unique because if you regard your learners as 'things' you will find it almost impossible to create learning. No two people have the same genetic sequence and identical life experiences; you are unique and your learners are unique. If you want to help people to learn effectively then both you and your students should feel good about these individual differences.

It is estimated that there are more potential neurone connections in the normal brain than there are molecules in the universe so there is no limit to learning potential. Everyone has so much spare brain capacity that the term 'ineducable' should not be a practical reality.

George Kelly (1955) said that we are 'not a victim of our own biography'. He meant that we can use our own internal construction of experiences and thinking to override the effect of our genetic inheritance and overcome the social learning of our upbringing and experience.

Classic writers have put forward the same idea. Rousseau, in *The Social Contract*, said that man is free but everywhere he is in chains and Bunyan's Christian, in *Pilgrim's Progress*, was locked in the Castle of Despair until he found that he had the keys to escape from his dungeon in his own pocket.

This is not a book about religious optimism although you should find the underlying theory optimistic. It is a book about how people learn and what can prevent individuals from reaching their optimum potential. The nature of personality and inheritance are discussed and the book will cover social learning and equal opportunities. There will be sections on self-image, the effect of learning in groups, communications and stress.

When you are responsible for helping other people to learn, the more you know about individuals and how to lessen the barriers to learning the better. Each person has an individual way of thinking which is called 'cognitive style'. Honey and Mumford (1982) have described four different learning styles – Activist, Reflector, Theorist and Pragmatist – which make a simple introduction to these complex ideas (see Chapter 9). The cognitive and humanistic learning theory from the first book in this series is a useful basis for this study of the unique and individual learner.

PERSONALITY

Although everyone is unique, have you noticed how people remain the same over many years and after a great many life experiences? This is not a question of our bodies maintaining exactly the same chemical molecules, because these are frequently changed throughout life. It is the genetic information in our cells which constantly changes the food we eat into our unique and characteristic cells; the consistency is fascinating. A little 2-year-old has a particular way of turning her head and will use the same gesture at the age of 22. The spacing between the eyes and the few hairs over the nose are the same on an old man's face as they were when he was a young chap going off to his first big school. Unique human beings have characteristics which are constant throughout life.

Personality has been described as the characteristic patterns of behaviour, thought and emotion which determine the way a person adjusts to the environment. Everyone has a continuous interaction with social and physical conditions and each one of us maintains a particular internal and external balance which is our unique personal style. Personality is everything which is typical of our own thoughts, words and deeds.

These characteristic patterns of behaviour are both external and internal. We have an external personality which is the person that other people observe and listen to, and an internal personality. The private personality contains all the fantasies and thoughts of our own inner eyes, ears and voices. This inside world is our own self-generated environment. We can use thinking and our working memory to contemplate our own subjective values and expectations.

What about the 'nature–nurture' argument? Is our personality determined by genes or by our upbringing? Few psychologists believe that personality is entirely predetermined by genetic inheritance because environmental conditions certainly account for some forms of human variation. On the other hand, few take the opposite view and believe that all human variation is due to environment. However, the effect of the nature–nurture balance on personality can influence our approach to learning and so this topic will be included with other aspects of personality when we think about helping individual (and naturally unique) people to learn.

JOHARI'S WINDOW

Two American psychologists called Jo and Harry gave their name to a model of personality which is very widely quoted; it is called 'Johari's window' (1970). The model has four areas of personality and a simplified version of the idea is shown in Figure 1.1.

	What I know about myself	What other people know about me
What other people know about me	**PUBLIC** to all A	**PUBLIC** to all but me B
What I know about myself	**PRIVATE** to me C	**UNKNOWN** to everyone D

Figure 1.1 *A simple version of Johari's window*

The top left-hand corner in the diagram represents what you know about yourself and what other people know about you. All these aspects of your personality are open to all.

The top right-hand corner in the diagram is an area of fear. You fear that everyone else may know something about you that you do not know yourself.

The bottom-left hand corner in the diagram is your own private world of thinking, planning and make believe.

The bottom right-hand corner represents your potential which noone knows about, not even yourself.

THE PUBLIC SELF

There is no need in the Johari model for the diagram to remain four even-sized squares. The more you push from left to right, the more you share with other people knowledge of your own personality; the more you push from top to bottom the more you reveal of yourself to the world and the more you discover about your own potential.

Let us have a look at these two movements in expanding public personality. The smaller we make the area which others know about ourselves and about which we are unaware, the better (this effect is shown in Figure 1.2). Removing this latent area of self-doubt makes us more content to 'live with ourselves'.

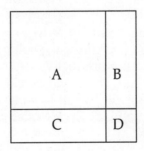

Figure 1.2 *Johari's window should become like this with maturity*

Success in human relationships depends on the extent to which we are prepared to share our private world with other people. Do not forget that when we have expressed our innermost thoughts to the outside world they have entered the world of public awareness. I think this is the reason for the phrase "'Til death us do part' in the wedding service. The only way we can retrieve privacy, once we have shared a thought, is by the death of that person. (By the way, the copy-editor for this book commented that 'This idea about "'Til death us do part" might be a little fanciful'. What a perfect example of the dangers of expressing your innermost thoughts too freely!)

⇨ **STOP AND REFLECT** ⇦

Do you sometimes express your thoughts and later wish that you had never opened your mouth?

Do you feel that you are giving a special gift to someone you love when you reveal your innermost thoughts?

Are you hurt when something told in confidence to a person is referred to in general conversation?

THE PRIVATE SELF

Memory is divided into a long-term storage system and a procedural memory for how we do things. I differentiate between day-dreaming and fantasy. Fantasy is the sort of thinking which starts with 'When I win the national lottery I will...'. This is good fun and a splendid way to go to sleep but it is not at all a productive use of time. Day-dreaming on the other hand, can be an excellent method of forward planning: 'Tomorrow, when I go out in the boat, I will take the tide down to Black Rock under engine to recharge the batteries and then I will take the forecast North Westerly wind round St Antony's Head and I should make Fowey by lunchtime'.

You do not have to carry out all the plans which you make in your private world but by this forward thinking you can make plans for coping with practical situations. When we come to deal with stress and anxiety, this method of anticipation will be the basis of learning coping skills for dangerous or new situations.

Personality includes every aspect of the person and this means our principles, beliefs and cultural standpoints. It is in our private world of personal thinking that we test out the effect of these factors too. Our moral viewpoint and opinions are tried out inside our heads before we declare them to the outside world. This is why it is especially difficult for youngsters: so many of their new individual viewpoints have to be sorted out and then experimented with for the first time.

ACTIVITY

Your own Johari window.
Take a sheet of paper and fill in each section of the diagram shown in Figure 1.3. Write down only what you suspect on the right-hand side and do the best you can. Remember to do the exercise in private and destroy the paper immediately you have finished! (I remember carrying out a practical which was also very self-revealing in a psychology workshop. After a few minutes the whole class of adults were hiding their papers with all the secrecy of little children. The lecturer was kind and pointed us in the direction of the office shredder when the practical was over.)

	What I know about myself	What other people know about me
What other people know about me	Record what is public	Speculate on what they may know
What I know about myself	Record what is private	Speculate on the unknown

Figure 1.3 *Make your own Johari's window*

Find out which aspect of your self-image is important

Before destroying the paper analyse what has been written into the four categories. Take each characteristic and place it under one of the following questions:

- Does this characteristic concern your academic, thinking or cognitive self?
- Does this characteristic concern your practical, skilled or competent self?
- Does this characteristic concern your feeling, emotional or intuitive sense?
- Does this characteristic concern your moral, spiritual or 'principled' self?

One of my friends found that she seemed to consider only academic values as a measure of herself and all other people. She literally had only one value for all the people she knew, including herself, and that was on the dimensions 'clever–stupid'! What a revelation this was to her about her own self-image.

SELF-IMAGE

An evenly-balanced, mature person should have some sort of coverage across all four general areas of personality, which can be called:

- *Cognitive* – the academic, thinking or mental self
- *Psycho-motor* – the practical, skilled or competent self
- *Affective* – the feeling, emotional or intuitive sense
- *Principled* – the moral, spiritual or believing self.

The first three should be familiar to anyone who understands the way in which Bloom (1964) classifies knowledge; I have added the fourth area as distinct from the affective domain. When I told one of my colleagues a story about a lecturer and his doubts about how anyone could be totally successful across all aspects of life, he suggested a fourth way in which a person could succeed; he said that a person could be spiritually successful. I am not sure that I agree with him but I have put it in for those who might find the idea useful.

If we are sensible we do not expect to have a high opinion of ourselves in each of these three or four areas. There is a distinction to be made between one's *ideal* self and one's real self; in areas where we do not feel that we have to compete too hard, we are quite happy to tolerate a large gap between the ideal and the real self without creating too much internal stress.

Look back to the second activity. Which of the areas are most important to you? Where did you concentrate your thoughts about what other people knew about you and what you thought about yourself? One or two areas should stand out; these are the areas which are important to you in your own self-image.

I fancy myself as a thinker: in my case the important area is cognitive. I don't contemplate entering the Olympics at my age and so my physical self is less critical in my self-image. When someone says, 'You are still overweight, Grannie', I do not mind too much; I comfort myself that I am still fit enough to do the things I want to do. However, when someone says to me 'Don't be stupid', my reaction is immediately to dish out a stinging reply and a cracking defence of my viewpoint.

We can identify ourselves by contemplation, study and reflection but most of the time our most effective feedback comes from other people. Whether we want it or not, other people are constantly reflecting their reactions to our behaviour, style and attitudes; this is sometimes called the *looking-glass self*. It is a mirror of ourselves and the reactions of other people can influence us strongly. I have often wondered what it must be like to be really pretty or really good-looking. Other people would always be glancing at me with admiration and approval; what an effect that would have on my self-image! No wonder beautiful people have such a self-satisfied air. I have noticed another thing about good-looking people: when old age eventually starts to erode their looks, they behave as if they have mislaid something. Generally we all receive constant feedback from other people on the state of our self-image.

When other people respond to us with negative reactions for reasons of general prejudice it is even more damaging to our self-image; not only does it give us room for doubt but it is also unjust because it is our sex, colour, ethnic or cultural background that is responsible and not our own individual personality. It is grossly unfair to me if I am called 'stupid' just because I am a woman and the negative criticism has nothing to do with an individual action of mine: I am helpless because I can do nothing to reverse the judgement. The same injustice is the basis of racism and the psychology of prejudice.

SELF-ESTEEM

The need for self-esteem is a motivating force for all normal human beings. For the learner the motivation can either be extrinsic, that is, coming from outside or intrinsic – coming from within. Self-esteem is one of the strongest motives found in training and teaching; that is why respect for other people is so vital to effective learning.

Extrinsic motivators

Teacher praise and approval is expressed in many ways: full-blooded verbal praise is rarely used outside the primary school and it can backfire if the learner suspects sarcasm. Normally an approving glance or an expressive 'umm' will be all that is needed for adults. Do not forget that in the behaviourism technique of intermittent reinforcement the student can be hooked on rare and infrequent praise just as some people are addicted to the constant playing of fruit machines. The fascination is never knowing when there is going to be a jackpot and so you keep having one more try just in case you are lucky next time. This is the basis of most superstitious behaviour. Good teachers sometimes play at being difficult to please in order to make learners try harder to earn a few crumbs of praise. I prefer to give lashings of praise for good work. The average age of my learners is 31 years, and older working people are often so beset with troubles that some enthusiastic praise does them the world of good.

A qualification can be an extrinsic motivator if it leads to more money, a better job or prestige amongst peers and contemporaries; there are however many other factors which might influence a learner.

The need for self-esteem is not always satisfied by striving for the 'good things' in life. Some people gain self-esteem by developing a reputation for being a nuisance or by demanding attention, even if that attention takes the form of punishment.

Intrinsic motivators

These are the self-esteem factors which come from within, and they are usually the best motivators for mature people who are self-starters. These are the people who were described as achieving 'self-actualization' in Maslow's (1970) hierarchy of needs. It is the most effective motivator and is very useful as an 'end state' for learning. People who take a pride in their own work and skills will enforce good quality practice standards upon themselves, they will set good standards for others and they will follow safe working practices.

This use of self-esteem as a guide to good practice seems an admirable guarantee for high quality work, but it can backfire if it develops into such pride in personal achievement that no learner can match up to the self-estimated standards. A trainer or teacher has to want the new learner to succeed in reaching a high standard of achievement, but sometimes a group of high achievers will close down entry to their 'club' to make it more exclusive. This happens when self-esteem hardens into distorted pride and it is not good for the learner.

PERSONALITY AND LEARNING

I hinted earlier that learning, competency and skills can become a part of personality. Can this be true? Think about people who follow a particular profession. My cousin Carol is a lawyer and a Scot. There is some part of Carol's personality which is the same as every other lawyer I have ever met. She is still a unique personality but there is something of the 'lawyer' which is a general characteristic. Her sister Margory is a medical doctor. She has lived in Canada for some time and a few of the Canadian attitudes have rubbed off on her personality but there is something about Margory's personality which is specific but still very like an awful lot of other highly-qualified medics.

What about teachers? My husband says you can tell them in the crowd by the way they inform everyone else without invitation; they say everything three times: they tell you what they are going to say, they say it, then they tell you what they have said. The habit drove him mad some time ago. Teachers are the only people who ask questions to which they think they have the answer. In general, it seems that what you learn gets internalized so that some of the learning becomes a part of your own personality.

Any professional ruling body lays down expected standards of behaviour and training for a full member of that profession. This is a deliberate attempt to shape individuals into a model of behaviour. There is always an initiation on entry even if the ceremonies have been blurred in modern times, and a member is in danger of being disgraced or discharged if any of the rules or traditions of the profession are broken. Thus someone who is active within a profession incorporates that learning and those skills into their own personality.

The section on intrinsic motivation suggested that some clubs or cliques make themselves exclusive and hard for newcomers to join, thus increasing the sense of value given to the learning. Learners who achieve skills, competency and knowledge will incorporate this learning into their own self-image.

ACTIVITY

Other people's self-image.
When you meet new people, say a new group of learners, by way of introduction ask them to describe

themselves and make a mental note of what they say first; if they are older take particular note.

You may well find that people first say how they earn their living – that is what they have learned – and this is particularly hard if you are unemployed. There is still the pressure to say something about how you earn a living, so the unemployed person will say, 'I am looking for work as a...'.

A challenge to our ability within the skill is a potentially dangerous threat to our self-image. I am a teacher and my aggressive reaction to anyone who says I am a bad teacher is forceful and serious because such a statement threatens my own self-image and self-esteem.

Recently, in the UK, many teachers and trainers have been putting together portfolios to show that they are competent assessors. Assessing is part of the skills of training and so a qualified trainer or teacher should be able to assess. This requirement to prove that you can do what everyone assumes you are able to do is a serious threat to self-image; the older and more experienced the trainer or teacher the greater is the threat. When someone tells a young learner that he or she cannot play the piano, the learner can shrug it off with a 'Who wants to play the piano anyway?' but tell teachers that they 'Can't teach' and the very basis of their personality is under attack.

Consider when this identification with learning starts to take place. One of my grandsons is keen on 'Kings and Queens'; at the age of 6 he is already something of an expert on the British monarchy at his school. He sees himself as an authority and one wonders if he will be a 'history' person for the rest of his life. His father certainly conceived a passion for nature at the same age and has grown up to be an outdoor, healthy but caring personality. My lifelong interest and qualifications in science might be attributed to an experiment I carried out with my brother when we lifted an old metal dustbin a considerable height off the ground by lighting a small syrup tin of household gas inside it. There is an expression, 'A little learning is a dangerous thing', but it seems that a little learning may have a lifelong effect on an individual's personality.

Chapter 2

Communications and Interpersonal Skills

➡ CONCEPTS ⬅

Social cognition
Learning by communicating
Verbal communication and listening
Non-verbal communication and observation skills
Written communication and the presentation of work
Transactional analysis
Negotiating
Teacher as counsellor

SOCIAL COGNITION

It is clear that self-image is strongly affected by other people's response to individual behaviour. Because learning comes from understanding and processing language and events which happen in the environment, it is important to look at how individuals respond to this social information about their behaviour. Some people seem unresponsive, insensitive and unaware of the reaction of others, some have such insight into other people's reactions and moods that it almost amounts to a sixth sense. This is called social cognition and there are five main ways in which we process social information about our own behaviour.

As a rational person

A rational person cannot tolerate two contradictory bits of information. For example, this information might be 'I smoke' and 'I know smoking causes lung cancer'. Given such contradictory evidence a rational person will find some reason to change one of the pieces of information so that he or she can become comfortable again. The response might be to give up smoking or to disbelieve the scientific evidence. For the person who responds as a rationalist this process of resolving dissonance continues as the incoming information is processed.

As a naive psychologist

Just as some people regard themselves as natural philosophers others think of themselves as natural psychologists. They attempt to analyse other people's reactions rather than to ask themselves if their own behaviour has caused the reaction. I find this form of self-confidence maddening and extremely arrogant; it is like meeting an eternal schoolmaster. This approach of 'Poor soul, what's the matter with you?' is the way some teachers process incoming social information.

As a data-processing trainee

This social ploy attempts to use scientific method and observation as a way of analysing human behaviour. It is the sort of approach which uses standard personality testing at an interview: in my view scientific method, developed for the physical sciences, is rather an inadequate tool for picking up all the delicate variations that can be found in human behaviour.

As a cognitive miser

Some people cannot be bothered to look at every new bit of information coming from outside, so they simply slot all new information into an existing memory box. This approach has three characteristics:

- priming – whatever was associated with the first occasion sticks
- prototype – all new people fit into an existing category
- anchoring – once the initial verdict is given, the opinion is never altered.

As a cognitive-affective human being

This approach uses all thinking processes which include emotions and intuition. The people wish their judgements to be softened and guided by feelings as well as by rational thoughts. This important area in learning is covered in Chapter 7.

⇨ **STOP AND REFLECT** ⇦

Can you think of examples of people known to you who fit into the five categories?

A rational person
A naive psychologist
A data processing trainee
A cognitive miser
A cognitive-affective human being

Which category do you think best describes your way of handling other people's communication?

How skilful are learners at using the information which comes to them from outside?

LEARNING BY COMMUNICATING

Language contains the concepts, facts, processes, attitudes and values associated with a particular subject. The learner must have good skills in understanding verbal and non-verbal communication as well as the ability to read the written word. Language is also important in thinking and memory and so the learner needs to be skilled in talking aloud and writing down ideas and thoughts so that active learning can take place. Students often say that they have to voice or speak aloud new words which express a new concept before they really get the hang of the idea; realization seems to come from this facility of owning the new thoughts.

Processes and methods are also part of learning and these depend on good listening and observational skills. Much communication is dependent on non-verbal signals. The learner must be skilled in observation and sensitivity to the subtle changes in meaning which are revealed by variation in tone and emphasis. Some general interpersonal skills are important for helping to understand individual learners and so they have been included in this chapter.

VERBAL COMMUNICATION AND LISTENING

These are some of the ways in which a learner will take part in verbal communication as a process of learning.

Teacher talk

The learner listens as the teacher puts forward his or her ideas, tells the learner what other people have thought, or generally passes the time of day. The learner has to learn the skill of paying attention and selecting useful parts of the teacher talk; once the verbal interaction between the teacher and the learner has started, the teacher will talk to clarify, explain and inform.

Teacher issuing instructions

This type of verbal communication is difficult to put across because details have to be slotted into the procedural memory and at the same time language has to be easily understood. The learner may have selective attention problems here.

Teacher asking questions

This form of verbal communication may be assessment when the teacher is checking on learning. It is one of the features of teaching that teachers often ask questions when they think they know the answers already. Sometimes teachers ask for the student's opinion.

Teacher building on learner's ideas

Teachers may agree or disagree with the student. They may seek clarification from the learner to make sure that a principle is understood or to gain information from the learner to help the rest of the group; it is in this area that verbal communication can be used to encourage active student learning.

Listening skills

There are four major levels of listening when a teacher is talking or instructing:

- skim listening – little more than awareness that someone is talking. Students pay attention only when they hear their own name or an unusual word (eg, swear words)
- surveying listening – the listener is trying to build a mental map of what is said, filtering out extraneous material and picking out the key steps or points of the argument
- search listening – active searching for specific information; waiting for a particular point to be made; following a certain line of discussion so that important but unexpected ideas may be filtered out
- study listening – deepest level of listening; hypothesizing about the speaker's thinking; developing the speaker's thoughts further.

Most people listen only intermittently and select only things of personal interest. It is very important that the learner tries to practise the skills of study listening because this is the way that learning can be maximized. Here is a list of suggestions for study listening techniques but you will have to work out your own methods for getting the most out of what another person is saying:

- Cut out all other communication channels. Concentrate on the speaker's voice and nothing else.
- Connect what he or she is saying directly to your own long-term memory and try to make the new information fit into examples from your own experience.
- Do not miss any detail and if you cannot place something immediately as a connection with your own experience, 'highlight' what was said for later thinking.
- Use the pauses or repetitions in the other person's delivery to store the new ideas which you have highlighted for later thinking.
- Really concentrate on what is going on and don't drift into reflection while raw, new material is coming into your own cognition.
- Remember that study listening is very hard work and you may have to ask for a break so that your own thinking can catch up. You do not want to suffer from information overload when such good material is being offered.

The trainer or teacher can think about their verbal communication with the learner and make sure that the presentation is suited to study listening.

ACTIVITY

Checklist for verbal presentations.
When preparing a verbal presentation, write a list of things that will encourage the learner to use study listening.

NON-VERBAL COMMUNICATION AND OBSERVATION SKILLS

We all say so much without using words. People are prepared to believe body language much more readily than the verbal communication. Body language is a popular topic for today's writers and television producers; in this chapter we will look at non-verbal communication from the point of view of the learner (Argyle, 1975).

Bodily contact

When I started to teach at my first further education college an old chemistry teacher gave me a word of warning. He said, 'Never touch a student'. In some respects this is good advice. Our multicultural society means that many teachers have groups from a wide variety of cultural backgrounds. Contact which is acceptable and seen as friendly by one student may be regarded as highly insulting by another, even to the point of being construed as sexual harrassment.

Can the student be helped to learn by physical contact? When learning some physical skills, it is possible to 'put' the student in the right position. In the caring professions, some physical comfort and physical lifting has to be learnt. Physical contact is an essential part of learning about beauty, hairdressing and aromatherapy. When bodily contact is an essential part of a skill the trainer has to teach the best way to approach a client. Permission has to be requested and given before physical contact is made. These skills can be therapeutic and beneficial to the client if they are carried out in a professional manner. The learning of body contact skills can be both challenging and rewarding.

Proximity

Have you noticed the way in which people contort themselves in order to avoid sitting nose-to-nose in a confined space? It is important to be aware of the effects of physical proximity upon learners. It can be even more embarrassing for you to have to return poor work to a student when you are both crammed into a small tutorial room.

The effect of proximity on communication is especially important to students from different ethnic backgrounds because there is a great difference in cultural norms. Germans and Americans generally like more space than the British, who like about the same space as people from Africa. People from some countries accept much smaller personal spaces and I find many of my students from China, the Middle East and Japan come too close to me for my idea of social comfort.

When you find your personal space is being invaded, the usual reaction is to turn yourself at right angles to the other person. This is a familiar technique which is practised on the London Underground or on any crowded bus or train. However, there is a danger in this strategy: because non-verbal communication is so powerful, evasive action which may be taken as a result of proximity can be interpreted as rudeness. Hostility can arise and neither the teacher nor the student may be aware of the cause of antagonism. If I am feeling threatened by an unusual proximity I find it is easier to explain to the student the idea of 'social space' rather than risk conveying an unspoken hostile message.

Posture

If you want to take over someone else's room or space, try standing by the door and leaning against the side of the open framework with one arm stretching as high as you can. A learner can be threatened by such an over-confident and dominating posture from a teacher. I use posture to manage the learning situation, so I stand up if I want to talk without interruption and I sit down and lean forward if I want to encourage the learner to talk; I sit on the floor, or at least bend under eye level, if I want to let the learners chat amongst themselves. All this non-verbal control is difficult for students to question. If I give a verbal command then they can argue, but when I command by posture most students don't work out what is going on!

Physical appearance

In technical and vocational teaching appearance may be a part of the skills which you are trying to pass on to your students – in some trades and vocations, physical appearance is part of the job. Many years ago I carried out some research on what various vocational teachers thought were the characteristics of good teachers. The science and technical teachers came up with such comments as 'logical', 'good at practical sessions' and 'knows the subject matter'; the teachers of business and professional studies favoured 'empathy' and 'good at communications', but the teachers from the commercial subject areas, such as hotel and catering, office studies, printing and photography suggested 'good looking', 'well-dressed' and 'charming'. In some areas of vocational training physical appearance may be very much part of the learning process.

Facial expressions

The face can express the six main emotions common to all human beings regardless of cultural or ethnic background. These emotions are:

- happiness ● surprise ● fear ● sadness ● anger
- disgust

The facial expression of these main emotions is unlikely to be misinterpreted by a learner but other sensations such as:

- interest ● pain ● startlement ● amazement
- questioning

have a local, cultural or national significance and the learner has to interpret these expressions correctly. If the learner gets it wrong it is surprising how different the message can become.

Classroom teachers should remember that their faces will be studied very intensively by the students; although teachers may feel that they have a poker-face very few people have completely expressionless features.

Gestures

These may be voluntary and conscious but many are involuntary and may or may not assist learning. There are three types of gesture which may be used in teaching:

- emblems
- illustrators
- self-touching.

Emblem gestures have a direct verbal translation. The finger waggle of 'Come here' and the palms exposed and open to the group, which means 'Peace' or 'I am honest', are two examples. Most emblem gestures are hand movements and they do have different meanings in different cultures. Beware of some gestures, especially those with two fingers or biting your thumbs!

Illustrator gestures can be useful. They help learning by:

- spatial movements – under or round, to go with words
- pictographs – showing shapes, say, a spiral staircase
- ideographs – like tracing a line of thought
- batons – showing tempo and rhythm.

But beware of pointing with the finger. A backward and forward motion of the index finger can mean 'I would like to stab you' and the index finger wagging up and down could mean 'I would like to beat you over the head'.

Self-touching gestures are not helpful to learning except to reveal to the learner a great deal about the teacher. Hiding parts of the body can indicate depression. Anxiety is shown in many ways, such as playing with the hair, opening and closing of the fists, wringing of the hands, plucking the eyebrows. Many of these gestures are not realized by the teacher and I have seen colleagues pick their noses and wipe their noses with their fingers quite openly and totally unwittingly in front of a large audience.

Direction of gaze

The teacher can help students to learn by focusing their attention on particular aspects of a presentation in order to highlight important parts. Where someone is looking can indicate what thought processes are taking place. The teacher can use student direction of gaze as feedback for student attention and interest.

Non-verbal vocalizations

Non-verbal techniques can be used in teaching to attract attention, maintain interest, highlight important parts of a lesson and generally add meaning to the discourse.

The pause can be very effective in verbal communication. After a question it encourages the students to strive for the answer, so helping memory and recall. Important points can be emphasized by increasing the loudness of the voice or by slowing down the pace of delivery. Such emphasis of speech can help learners to learn.

WRITTEN COMMUNICATION AND THE PRESENTATION OF WORK

Learners vary in their ability to master the written word. Let us look at how learning is affected by these skills.

Reading formal textbooks

One excellent system for reading a textbook is called the PQRST method and was first proposed by R P Robinson in 1970 (see Atkinson *et al.*, 1993). Here are his stages:

- Preview – skim through the entire chapter and read the summary at the end carefully to see which topics are covered and how the book is organized.
- Question – turn the main topics into a short series of questions like, 'What are the main ideas that the author is trying to cover in this section?'
- Read – do not read more than 10 to 15 per cent of the words but fast read each section to answer the questions posed in the Q stage.
- Self-recitation – after each section make yourself repeat the main points of the section, either on paper or inside your head.

- Test – at the end of the section make yourself write down the main points from each section in the chapter.

There are many other techniques for reading for information but I find this a good system. For reading references a learner must master the information technology systems which are available in the library and in resource centres. There has been a massive explosion of input but the systems for information search are now much more effective and efficient than before.

Preparing for written work

Reading is only one skill used in the preparation of written work. There are sub-skills such as grammar, spelling, structure, logical presentation, word usage and general powers of expression. The writing should be planned to illustrate original thought and an overall grasp of the subject. The management of time and work effort is an important part of writing.

Presenting written work

Once upon a time the pressure of time limits was used as an excuse for poor written presentation in formal examinations. Recall and the marshalling of facts were seen as so important that writing and presentation skills often took second place; nowadays formal examinations are frequently only part of the assessment process. Learners are now expected to demonstrate an ability to present clear evidence of what they have learnt, in portfolios of evidence, assignments and reports. There is a clear obligation for the student to 'sell' a completed assignment to the assessor or verifier. Advances in wordprocessing and personal computers have allowed many techniques to become widely available. Printing, layout and other techniques, which used to be the sole concern of the printer, are becoming common skills.

This change in technology and the general availability of materials have put a lot of pressure on the learner. I can't see any limit to the need for these presentation skills;

indeed, there could be an increase in the demands placed on students as multi-media technology becomes more widely available.

TRANSACTIONAL ANALYSIS

Eric Berne (1968) wrote a book called *Games People Play*. It is fun to read and it has had a lasting effect upon the study of interpersonal behaviour. Berne introduced the idea of transactional analysis and he analysed the different ways in which we react to each other. This work is very useful for understanding how interactions between learners and the teacher may develop.

There are five different ego states which a person might adopt. Let us speculate how they can affect the behaviour of the learner and the teacher.

Critical parent

If a teacher takes the role of a critical parent he or she can quickly upset the learner, especially if the learner is mature. I have seen one teacher lose control of a whole class simply by calling them 'Gels'. Equally, teachers quickly resent any learner adopting a critical parent approach. No teacher likes to be patronized by a learner!

Nurturing parent

This can be quite a helpful approach for the teacher, especially if the learners are younger and not very confident. The caring mother or father figure is not too inappropriate in some learning situations but it should not be allowed to get out of hand. Again, a teacher usually resents any attempt by the learner to patronize.

Adult

In an 'adult' ego state a person takes a calm, mature approach to interaction. The voice and non-verbal communications are appropriate for serious discussion. The language and thoughts are calm and well-balanced. If both the learner and the teacher adopt this ego state then the most effective learning climate is created.

Natural child

Stormy, violent and impulsive behaviour is unsuitable for learners and even more disastrous for the teacher. Teachers who behave like children do not last long, yet constantly I see grown men and women reverting to very childish behaviour as soon as they are given the chance to become learners again. To put it kindly, it may be something to do with the release from heavy responsibilities that makes some adult learners become silly and irresponsible.

Adaptive child

This ego state does not represent real childish behaviour but an attempt to whine and wheedle in order to influence other people. The non-verbal behaviour may take the form of flirting and pouting and the verbal behaviour can be a series of silly phrases. Freud had a lot to say about ego defence mechanisms and this manifestation of regression is a clear example. Certainly it is unhelpful behaviour for both the teacher and the learner.

ACTIVITY

Recognizing and correcting unhelpful responses.
Inappropriate responses do not have to be extreme in order to hamper learning. Practise looking at interactions between people. Try to recognize the five ego states so that you can intervene with an adult response; you may find that you can draw another person into more mature, and thus more productive, behaviour.

NEGOTIATING

Modern programmes for education and training involve much more individual agreement in the planning of course work and study. Teacher and learner enter into negotiation when an action plan or a learning contract is being agreed. Here are some general points for successful negotiation:

- ask questions until you are sure of the main objective
- look at the pros and cons of each proposal
- do not allow anyone to take up a fixed position
- be honest and say what you feel
- be constructive in disagreement
- do not get bogged down in minor detail
- listen to the other person
- keep summarizing the progress achieved so far
- do not be personal
- do not exaggerate
- do not make a case out of one example
- keep asking questions to make sure that everything is covered
- be prepared to bring all points to a conclusion
- be prepared to make firm decisions
- give all parties a record of what has been agreed.

TEACHER AS COUNSELLOR

To help learners to learn, teachers often have to act as counsellors; this may mean negotiating with the learner, reviewing the work so far and may involve handing out negative criticism. Learners can feel insecure and resent adverse criticism if the teacher appears to be inept. John Heron (1986) has described six different 'interventions' which can take place between a client and a practitioner; teacher and learner interactions fit successfully into the scheme. In this model there are three types of intervention which are authoritarian and three types of intervention which are facilitative. All of them are useful in some aspect of teacher/learner interaction and I have simplified John Heron's work so that it applies to teachers alone:

- *Authoritarian interventions:*
  - prescriptive: the teacher advises and prescribes a course of action to the learner
  - informative: the teacher gives out information to the learner
  - confrontational: the teacher criticizes a learner's work or performance.
- *Facilitative interventions:*
  - cathartic: the teacher lets the learner express emotions as a release
  - catalytic: the teacher stimulates the learner's own work and ideas
  - supportive: the teacher gives practical support to the learner's work.

All trainers and teachers inform but at times we are called upon to carry out each of the other interventions. One of the skills we are often not very good at is handing back unsatisfactory work without arousing resentment and hostility in the learner. The secret of confrontation is to criticize the work and not the person; then you can get together with the learner as a facilitator and catalyse some better work. Probably all teachers and trainers have experience of support for the weaker learner but many will have difficulty accepting that the release of strong and disturbing emotions is a proper function of the trainer or teacher's role.

Interpersonal skills are so important to learning because they enable the trainer and teacher to handle their own and the learner's emotions. Chapter 7 gives more coverage of emotions and the affective domain.

Chapter 3

Learning in Groups and the Effect of an Audience

➡ **CONCEPTS** ⬅

Formation of learning groups
Communication within groups
Types of groups
Social facilitation for the learner
Roles within a group
Group dynamics
Aims and ojectives of learning groups

FORMATION OF LEARNING GROUPS

Just after the Gulf war, in the late 1980s, my students found the stages of group formation easy to remember. I have put a note at the end of this chapter to explain what it was that jogged their memories. Here are the stages of group formation:

● *Forming* – at this stage everyone feels anxious because they do not know how to behave or what is expected of them. The first task is to establish rules and decide what methods are to be used.

- *Storming* – there is conflict between sub-groups as individuals oppose group pressure and opinions become polarized, the usefulness of the task is questioned, and everyone tends to react emotionally.
- *Norming* – group work begins to harmonize and find a common purpose, norms are established and members of the group start to support each other. A communication system develops within the group.
- *Performing* – the group begins to carry out constructive work, they start to channel their energy towards the task in hand, and individuals can make use of their expertise. Satisfactory results appear.
- *Informing* – the group turns to reports and set assignments; this is the stage of reporting progress and achievement to outsiders. A learning group will hand their work to assessors and verifiers.

The standard stages of group formation apply to all learning groups such as group tutorials or portfolio workshops. Nowadays, active learning is a popular strategy in teaching and training, and learning support groups are encouraged because individuals can find encouragement and help when working with others on the same learning task. This method of learning is called 'peer support' but it is important to remember that the learning groups need time to establish themselves before useful learning can be achieved. If you want to set up a learning group it is important to make sure that the group know the stages of group formation and are encouraged to stick together so that the group becomes an effective learning unit.

COMMUNICATION WITHIN GROUPS

The teacher or trainer sets the rules for a group formation and chooses the communication network within the group which has a strong influence on the type of learning. Four different types of networks are described below.

Everyone can communicate with everyone else

Sometimes this can result in a lively, open discussion but all too often such freedom of communication leads to a meaningless 'talking shop'. Forceful and attention-seeking people dominate all conversation; bullying personalities override the discussion with the second-rate and unimportant. This is a suitable place to put in one of my favourite ideas: 'Truth has nothing to do with being in the majority'. Trainers and teachers should think carefully about open group discussion as a method for helping people to learn. A great deal of time can be wasted unless firm control and guidance is applied; you have to face the fact that the collective opinions and ideas of a group may not be worth airing.

Restricted open communication within a group

There are some interesting ideas for group learning in this category. I have seen the 'Quaker meeting' rules work extremely well in a large learning group. The rules are:

Each person can speak only once in the session.
Nobody can 'follow on' from another person's statement.
Silence is strictly maintained by all except the individual who is speaking.

There are many variations, such as allowing each person to speak in strict rotation, but the insistence on silence seems to encourage thought and consideration of other people's ideas.

Individuals discuss with immediate neighbours

The 'buzz group' has an effective learning function: it gives the learner an immediate opportunity to try out new words and ideas. This talking aloud seems to help individual learners to feel that they own new information. It is of no consequence if the teacher doesn't hear and thereby loses the chance to correct any errors: the importance of letting everyone take part far outweighs the advantage of immediate feedback. Large groups are not suitable for discussion and the exhibitionists who sing out questions in big lectures should be discouraged because they can waste a lot of learning time for the other students.

Snowballing or pyramid networks

This is a good introductory method for establishing new learning groups and as a communication network it is a splendid way to give each individual an active role in the learning group. The whole group is given some question to discuss, or information to collect, and they are told to find someone else to work with as a pair. After a time the pairs are told to move on to fours and this doubling process can continue as long as practicable; sometimes it is possible to go on doubling up until the whole learning group is reassembled.

TYPES OF GROUPS

There are three principal types of learning group:

- *Authoritarian* – the traditional organization with a teacher firmly in charge. Clear group rules. Passive learners who are expected to do what they are told to do.
- *Democratic* – student-centred methods and organization with a negotiated programme and active learning methods.
- *Laissez-faire* – little direction or planning for learning from the teacher or trainer. Individual learners are expected to be responsible for their own learning and to plan their own programme of study.

Much scorn has been poured on traditional (authoritarian) teaching methods in the last few years, but I think that there are occasions when this approach to group learning is useful and suited to the subject in hand. I have observed up to a hundred teaching and training sessions each year for 25 years and I have interfered and stopped a lesson only once. The occasion was a *laissez-faire* practical on organic chemistry which I stopped before the students were blown up. There are occasions when strict class control is essential for health and safety.

Democratic learning groups are in line with current teaching theory and are strong on motivation and learning method; this approach should probably be considered first but not regarded as the only type of effective possibility.

Few learners are sufficiently mature, motivated and autonomous to benefit from a *laissez-faire* approach. In practice, freedom is very difficult to handle and most learners need support and encouragement; this is a problem for all open learning and resource centres. Only a few leave school, college or university as self-starting learners and yet the ultimate aim for every person is considered by many educationalists and psychologists as achieving autonomy in learning.

SOCIAL FACILITATION FOR THE LEARNER

At the end of the nineteenth century, early psychological experiments showed that little children pedalled faster on bicyles when they were being watched by an audience. An American experiment where the researchers used one-way mirrors in a pool hall appeals to me. Privately they observed the regular players and divided them into two groups – those who were above average and those who were below. Then the researchers joined the players on the floor of the hall and stood around watching the games; they did not comment on the play but simply watched. These games were then compared with the first observations and it was found that, when watched, the above average got better and the below average got worse.

The effect of an audience is the desire for sensation on the part of the players. The effect is common to athletes, actors, sportsmen and women and it applies to students and teachers too. Sometimes an audience improves performance and sometimes it inhibits the performer, but a professional is always improved. There are three important factors which influence the effect of an audience, described below.

Number of people

A small number of people does not have the same effect as a large audience. Learners don't seem to mind speaking up when a few people are standing round at a demonstration but they may become tongue-tied when faced with a group of 20 or 30. The size of audience seems to affect teachers and trainers too. Many workshop and classroom teachers who are confident and effective with a group of 20 or 30 freeze when they are expected to address 200. I call this 'main hall nerves'.

Proximity

We have seen that social space is important. It is also an important factor in the audience effect, in that closeness of other people can be quite daunting. Inexperienced lecturers, for example, will cling onto any object that they can put between themselves and the audience; they will often clutch their notes, the lectern or the overhead projector to distance themselves from the other people.

Importance of observers

When you are asked to perform in front of people who you know very well, the audience should present little threat. The learning group should feel a safe place for the learner. It becomes a question of trust: each person must be confident that he or she can try out ideas and express personal views without the risk of ridicule, blame or punishment. Learning openly within a group is very effective, especially for individual confidence. It may be the first chance that learners have to prove to themselves that they 'can really deliver the goods'.

The powerful audience effect on learners can prove difficult when external examiners and verifiers are involved. The very presence of an important audience affects the performance. Fear of failure can reduce and inhibit the performance of some, while people with drive and the expectation that they will succeed can come out well in such a test (see 'Achievement motivation' in the first book in this series).

Putting learners together

Some interesting work has been done on the facilitation of learning by putting learners in pairs. Here are some examples of the effect:

With someone who is a little better...
an excellent learning effect;
the improvement seems achievable.

With someone a little worse...
little effective learning;
all rather boring.

With someone who is vastly superior(1)...
if there is no helpful coaching then
a complete turn-off.

With someone who is vastly superior(2)...
with encouragement this
can be a wonderful learning opportunity.

Putting poor performer with poor performer...
can be quite useful because
they may help and encourage each other.

Much has been written about competition versus collaboration. Again I am happy to use both approaches because I think that both can be used to help the learner. The choice of method should not be a question of personal dogma; rather, the teacher may follow these well-tried guidelines:

If the task is *simple* and needs to be *well-learnt*: competition between learners encourages improvement.

If the task is *complex* and *difficult to learn*: competition discourages progress in learning and collaboration is much more effective.

ROLES WITHIN A GROUP

The theory about general group roles applies well to the roles within learning groups. Let's see how these roles affect the learner and other group members.

Specific status

An acknowledged expert has a special status within the group. This may be the teacher or trainer and be accorded on the basis of expert knowledge of the subject. (This is the idea of 'an authority' which we will look at in the next chapter.) Sometimes learners within a group have specific status by virtue of their employment or previous experience. It is something to watch out for in adult learning groups. The wise teacher and trainer checks on the background of the learning groups to make sure that they are not embarrassed by sudden expertise coming unexpectedly from the group. I remember an occasion when I had been teaching navigation to a group for some weeks before I found out that one of them had already sailed round the world!

Diffuse status

Inequalities in status can come about through such factors as race, cultural background, age or gender. Stereotypes may suggest that men are more dominant, assertive and competent than women; middle-class learners seem to have more status than those from the working class. These stereotypes may cause diffuse status within the learning group and affect role expectation. Diffuse status may make group learning less effective because there may be a tendency to listen to a man because he is a man, even though he does not have a clear grasp of the topic, rather than a woman who does have clear insight into the topic. These factors arise in learning and it is for this important reason that we will look at prejudice and its effect on equal opportunities.

Social loafing

If there is lack of identity within the group then an individual may 'drop out' of the proceedings. Think of a large tug-of-war team. The more people there are, the less likely it is that everyone will pull his or her weight – it is easy to take a breather in the middle of a crowd. The building of group morale and a good atmosphere can help each individual feel needed and valued in the learning group.

Task roles

The function of the learning group determines its optimum size. Sometimes a large number of tasks will need to be performed and a larger group will be better, but if the size of the group is increased then there is proportionately less time for individual contributions. Another disadvantage of a large group is the possibility of social loafing, so the optimum size is the smallest number that can perform all the necessary tasks.

Maintenance roles

Within any working group some members have to fulfil roles which assist the smooth running of the group. Groups need people who are prepared to encourage, harmonize and summarize as the work of the group progresses.

Anti-group roles

Some group members are not content simply to be idle: they like to take an active and antagonistic role. Individuals may use a group for their own personal benefit. Basically this attempt to dominate group work is an attention-seeking device but it is a very irritating and time-wasting habit.

The devil's advocate

Far from being anti-group, this role is essential for making sure that the group does not come to bad decisions through the misuse of mutual encouragement. Sometimes a closed group will egg itself on to make more extreme decisions than individual members of the group would make on their own. Irving Janis (1982), an American psychologist, described this effect of 'group-think'. He pointed out how important it is to have an appointed and respected devil's advocate so that senior government policy cannot be exposed to bad decision-making; the same argument applies to learning groups.

Leadership

This role may belong to the teacher or appear from within the learning group. There are two types of leadership which may be chosen to encourage learning when the teacher takes on this role:

- Concentrating on the learning task, the teacher or trainer:
  - makes his or her attitude clear
  - rules with an iron hand
  - criticizes poor work
  - speaks in a manner which will not be questioned
  - assigns particular tasks
  - maintains standards of performance
  - encourages the use of uniform procedures
  - makes sure that the targets for a course are understood
  - makes learners follow standard rules and procedures
  - lets learners know what is expected of them
  - makes learners work to full capacity
  - sees that all the work is coordinated.

- Concentrating on the learner's own needs, the teacher or trainer:
  - treats all learners as equal
  - strives to make him or herself easy to understand
  - listens to all learners
  - is willing to make changes
  - is friendly and approachable
  - makes the learners feel at ease
  - puts the learners' suggestions into effect
  - obtains the learners' approval before going ahead.

I am sure that both approaches are useful in different learning situations. If I was helping pharmaceutical students to learn I would use a task-oriented approach. Because they are preparing to work in a dispensary for the general public, my objective would be to ensure that my students got the medicines right every time! If I were training individuals to act independently on their own initiative then I would adopt the second approach.

ACTIVITY

Roles within a group

Here is an activity to help even the most boring meeting to pass with interest and amusement. Bales (1950) suggested the roles which an individual may adopt in any group meeting (see below). Some individuals may use more than one role.

Draw up a grid and place the names of your group along the top and the following roles down the left-hand side of the sheet. You can then fill in the grid at leisure throughout the meeting. It can be seen as an anti-group activity, so keep the paper to yourself! Here are the roles which you can cross-reference with the people at your meeting:

Task roles:
- initiator
- information-giver
- information-seeker

Group maintenance roles:
- coordinator
- encourager
- harmonizer
- standard-setter
- follower

Anti-group roles:
- blocker
- recognition-seeker
- dominator
- avoider.

GROUP DYNAMICS

Some of the characteristics of successful learning groups are described in this section.

Developing trust

If there is a shared responsibility between group members and all the members are acting in a natural way, then the group is working well. Effective groups face up to problems and expect to be successful; they set realistic goals and achieve them.

Cohesiveness

Successful learning groups are usually happy to tackle the same types of task and they like each others' company. This homogeneity is an essential feature of good group work: it is clear that people who share similar characteristics and have shared experience get on better together. Long and successful relationships are usually based on the pairing of similar people, an important point to remember when we look at equal opportunities. The student experience at the University of California shows that given completely free choice, people form alliances by race, age, sex, social status, attitudes or values.

⇨ **STOP AND REFLECT** ⇦

Does cohesiveness come about because the choice was made before the group was formed? Or does the common group experience draw people together?

Atmosphere

Some buildings and places seem to exude a feeling of happy and successful learning. It is almost as if the previous groups of students have worn and warmed the seats, walls and rooms so that a mellow feeling spreads to the learners now in occupation. These special places don't have to be very grand; in fact they are often rather tattered and old.

I have always paid great attention to the stage management of group learning. Physical surroundings and good housekeeping set the scene for undisturbed hard work and concentration.

Learners feel confident and secure in well-worn and familiar surroundings; teachers and trainers can create their own confidence-building surroundings. New learners obey the unwritten rules and preserve a cooperative atmosphere. Reorganization and change have destroyed many established institutions; modern managers do not seem to appreciate that it takes time to build a centre of learning excellence and that atmosphere is an important aid to learning.

Standards

Good learning groups maintain high standards. There are five areas in which high standards are important:

- *work* – using the best and easiest methods, dictating how fast, how long and with which safety considerations the work is to be done
- *attitudes* – sharing a common interpretation of past and present approaches
- *interpersonal behaviour* – shared routines and timetables; predictability reduces group conflict
- *style* – this may be a common clothes style, common language or slang
- *morals* – clear guidelines on ethical practice such as telling the truth and equal opportunities.

These factors do lead to effective groups and tend to maintain the status quo. For the learner this stability usually has a positive effect on learning. However (to misquote Tennyson), 'the old order changeth yielding place to new, lest one good habit should corrupt the world'. Keep an eye on all this complacent good practice because there is a danger of becoming fixed in one approach and you may miss better and more effective methods.

AIMS AND OBJECTIVES OF LEARNING GROUPS

I have already made the point that the aims can be task-oriented or of socio-economic use to the learner. Here are two lists of intrinsic and extrinsic objectives which show how the two learning aims can be linked:

INTRINSIC

Task	*Socio-economic*
Enjoying the subject	Greater sensitivity to others
Judging ideas	Judging self
Examining assumptions	Encouraging self-confidence
Listening attentively	Personal development
Tolerating ambiguity	Tolerating ambiguity
Learning about groups	Awareness of others' strengths and weaknesses

EXTRINSIC

Task	*Socio-economic*
Follow-up to lecture or demonstration	Giving support
Understanding handouts	Arousing interest
Improving relationships	Evaluating own feelings
Gauging progress	Identifying with others

All these possible outcomes of learning help to develop the learner and encourage personal growth which can be summed up as:

● developing communication skills and thinking

- developing personal confidence
- managing your own learning
- working with others
- gaining insight into yourself and others.

Note on group formation

The stages of group formation are forming, storming, norming, performing and informing. The name of the military operation in the Gulf war was 'Desert Storm' and the name of the American officer commanding was H. Norman Schwarzkopf. In the popular press the commander was known as 'Stormin' Norman'. Isn't it amazing how quickly memories of vital events fade! What used to be a really good and memorable tip for learning has completely lost its currency and use.

Chapter 4

The Learner's Rights

PRINCIPLES WHICH AFFECT THE LEARNER

Many learners are unaware of the principles which affect their learning. Here is an example. When the Open University was beginning to develop, many years ago, it allowed graduates from other universities to take what were called 'post-experience' courses. Keen to see how the Open University system worked, I enrolled for the first course in my subject. After a few weeks I found that I was studying a one-year course in Marxist biochemistry. I was amazed; in fact I still have difficulty in believing it unless I pull down a first edition of a paperback course book from my bookshelf and start to read it again. There is no doubt that some parts of biochemistry do lend themselves very well to communist ideology.

⇨   **STOP AND REFLECT**   ⇦

Do you think about the underlying principles which may affect what you learn or what you teach?

Have you had a sudden insight into factors which affect your work?

Have you thought about who is influencing the subject matter which you learn or teach?

There are underlying principles which guide what we learn, how we learn it and what we are intended to learn. Even if we are not aware that such principles exist, we are still influenced by them and it just means that someone else is pulling the strings.

There is nothing sinister implied; it is only a statement of the obvious fact that there are always underlying principles behind human activity. What is important is that the learner should know which principles are accepted in their system, then they can make a fuss if they feel that their rights are being infringed.

Throughout this chapter I will suggest 'learner's rights' as I develop the arguments. The suggestions are summarized in the Activity at the end of the chapter so that you can decide which rights are appropriate for your learners and for yourself. Let us look at some of the possible principles which may be involved and then attempt to define the learner's rights and our responsibilities as well.

THE PURSUIT OF SCIENTIFIC TRUTH

It can be claimed that anyone who publishes a book or a research paper intends that other people should learn from it. Should scientific researchers be allowed to continue in the headlong pursuit of science? Historically, scientists have been muzzled before. Think of the shock-horror when someone suggested that the world was round or that man was descended from apes. This debate on the right to pursue scientific truth is really bubbling as I write.

⇒ **STOP AND REFLECT** ⇐

Do you think the human foetus should be used in research into infertility?

Do you think animals should be used in research into human ill-health?

Do you think there should be research into the physiology of humans from different sexes or racial groups?

Think of the violent reaction there would be if the scientists were to discover that there was a physiological difference between most women's brains and most men's brains. This would be totally unacceptable to many. There are signs in current research that this has already been suggested; it is one of the many such issues currently under discussion.

Professional bodies are well aware of the need to guide members on underpinning ethical issues. For example, I am a graduate member of the British Psychological Society and my own research has to fit into the strict guidelines which are laid down by the BPS. When I am teaching psychology I have to make sure that all the students are aware of the BPS guidelines before they start on their project work. Guidance may be given at a national level; for example, the Secretary of State for Education in Britain has recently issued a Learner's Charter for Further Education and a Learner's Charter for Higher Education (see the end of the chapter).

There are several principles which guide the process of learning. Fundamental to any debate on the content of what we teach is the learner's right to know the truth. This is one principle you may consider in the Activity at the end of the chapter.

THE NATURE OF AUTHORITY

There are three ways in which we use the idea of authority in everyday language. These are, 'an authority', 'in authority' and 'authoritarian'. How can each meaning be applied within the fields of training and education?

The teacher as an authority

This meaning of the idea of authority applies to a particular person. It is used to describe people who have studied, worked and practised in a subject until they know a great deal about it. You might be an authority, for example, on the internal combustion engine, on the running of small businesses or on early English music.

A while ago, many would-be teachers tried to become an authority in their chosen subject area in the hope of being employed as a teacher. Nowadays most teachers and trainers aim to be 'facilitators of learning'. Learning time is spent on action plans, coaching, work experience, review and assessment and not so much in a classroom listening to the 'authority'.

Perhaps this swing to active learning has gone a little too far. The trainer and teacher might reconsider if they are an expert in any area of knowledge. Learning is the deliberate intention of an educational or training programme, which means that the teacher must know in which direction the learner is heading. Surely, initially the teacher must know more than the student on the particular subject or know where other expertise can be found?

I think the students have a right to expect that the trainer or the teacher is *an authority* in their particular subject area.

⇨ **STOP AND REFLECT** ⇦

Are you such an enthusiast in your own area of interest that you read all the latest publications?

Do you spend your spare time practising what you teach?

Do you belong to any organization in which you can discuss your subject with colleagues?

Are there 'in-service' training facilities that you could use?

The teacher in authority

In the last section I made the statement that 'Learning is the deliberate intention of an educational or training programme'. Some learning can be quite unintentional. I can peer through a hole in the fence on a building site and have a good lesson on how to mix concrete without the building labourer being aware that I am learning anything.

Educational and training programmes are different. Here there must be a deliberate intention that learning will take place. What is to be learned is deliberately set down in the form of aims and objectives. Whatever the programme, someone or somebody has overall authority for the learning and this authority is exerted at several levels. Some of the examples are:

- National government, with responsibility throughout the country
- Local government, with responsibility in a geographical area
- Trade, commercial or professional associations, with responsibility in a vocational area
- Independent institutions, with responsibility for specific programmes.

When we, as teachers and trainers, put these schemes into effect we have the authority of one of these bodies to support us. We are representatives of the overall authority; for our particular group of learners we are *in authority* over their learning.

This responsibility to represent some wider authority is probably expressed as part of our conditions of employment or hire. It may be a job description for the sort of work that we agree to carry out as a part of our contract.

Because we are *in authority*, the learner has the right to expect us to know the regulations and procedures which will result in the successful completion of the programme. I think that the learners should be confident that they will be successful under our care.

The teacher as authoritarian

This third meaning of authority is descriptive of the style of presentation of learning material. For example, I can teach in a democratic way with plenty of discussion about the student's wishes. On the other hand, I might choose an authoritarian approach and insist on complete silence and attention to my words at all times. There are times when one particular method may be the best way to help learning.

FREEDOM AND AUTONOMY

Because most people go on learning informally throughout their adult lives, a realistic aim for all formal learning is that the learner should learn to become autonomous. This means that learners are free from dependence on other people for their learning and they are able to pursue their studies without assistance. When I was at university, this learning 'how to learn' was a legitimate aim of what was otherwise a period of gentle self-indulgence. As a result of my university experience I was supposed to learn to become a self-starter in learning. This did not mean that I never needed other people to help my learning and I certainly needed other people's ideas and thoughts in written and spoken forms but I was expected to instigate, plan and guide my own study.

There is another aspect to autonomy which is very important for the freedom of the individual: by further study and reflection, I should be able to change my mind about anything that I have learnt so far. Although I may have strong principles, ideas and beliefs, I should be capable of changing my mind on everything. If this is the case, then I have truly learnt and I have not been indoctrinated. I hope that this is true of my own learning because it is an ideal that I admire; sadly, there is always room for doubt because one can never be sure that one possesses such independence of thought!

Whether these ideals are attainable or not they do make sound objectives to aim at in our own learning and they make good aims for our students as well. As a statement of learner's rights this idea may be expressed as:

> The student has the right to expect to achieve independence in learning.

Now we have a more difficult question. Do learners have the right to freedom while they are learning to be independent and autonomous?

⇨ **STOP AND REFLECT** ⇦

Should students be allowed to choose ignorance?

There are some skills, like reading or numeracy, which are so basic to all other learning, that we can ask the question, do students have the right not to achieve fundamental learning skills?

Do you, as a teacher or trainer, have the right to give an easier and simpler explanation which will make it extremely difficult for the learner to progress towards a deeper understanding of a subject?

This dilemma has many parallels in modern living. How far should I force someone to do something against his or her will? There may good grounds for believing that what I want them to do is in their best long-term interests. I can try persuasion and guile but ultimately in a democratic society I must decide that the freedom of the individual is the overriding principle.

I do not believe that teachers should avoid responsibility in this direction. Perhaps this argument for a learner's right can be summed up as follows:

> The right of learners to expect the teacher to work in the learners' best long-term interests as far as these interests are agreed and understood is certainly a principle which needs to be considered.

RESPECT FOR PERSONS

Any learner beginning any programme or course enters into a learning contract; it is almost always an unwritten contract but it is an agreement nevertheless.

⇨ **STOP AND REFLECT** ⇦

Do you expect the learner to listen to what you say?
Do you expect the learner to take your advice about learning?
Do you expect your learner to believe what you say?
Do you expect the learners to behave in such a way that they don't interfere with other people's learning?

You may not be able to give clear and simple answers to these questions but in a real sense learners surrender their own freedom of action and independence to the authority of the teacher. Learners assume, for example, that they have a duty to answer a teacher's questions as honestly and as accurately as possible. It is important that teachers do not abuse this unwritten contract and exceed the limits of their privileged position. For example, students may squirm and feel ashamed in class under the verbal sarcasm of an unsympathetic teacher.

Learners have the right to expect to be treated with respect by their teachers and trainers and you may wish to include this principle in your list.

EQUALITY

This principle has many applications in education and training. It becomes very complex when we ask when, where and to whom the principle of equality should be applied. This quote from Aristotle can serve as a guide to discussion of equality:

> It is as unfair to treat unequals equally
> as it is
> to treat equals unequally.

Are individuals equal in the talents that they have inherited genetically?

Clearly not. Some people are tall and springy and have an advantage in high jumping. Some people have good co-ordination and quick reactions so that they would have a greater chance of becoming good at Formula One racing. Some people have an introverted nature and enjoy thinking deeply and reflectively about mental problems and are suited to heavy academic study. Some people have a musical ear, good hand-eye coordination and memory so that they become first-rate musicians.

Obviously training and study can improve the performance of a jumper, the Formula One driver, the academic and the musician but I think it is fair to say some genetic basis in the first place is essential for a person to reach mastery of any one of these skills. This is a big debate. Can a person master a skill by teaching and training alone or do they have to have some innate, natural talent? This is called the 'nature-nurture' argument and it has raged for years; some people are very persistent and may even use the advice that they are unsuited for a task as a spur for motivation and success! However, even the most hardened 'progressive' educationalist would admit that successful learning depends on a measure of inherited natural attributes because it seems so unfair if you put the argument round the other way. It is what I call the 'hard on parents' argument. Suppose you believe that only training and upbringing affect a person's success, then when a son or daughter fails to succeed they can place all the blame on their parents.

This set of suggestions can be stated as:

The right of the learners to special training and education where they have naturally inherited, educationally important advantages or disadvantages.

This covers people who start from a clearly different position. It means that the musical have the right to the sort of musical education which is not open to all. The young ballet dancer has the right to ballet school. The person with a physical barrier to learning has the right to special training and help to reduce or remove that barrier to learning.

Should there be equal opportunity for access to training and education for everyone?

Clearly there ought to be equal access for all in a democratic society. The principle is consistent:

The learner has the right to equal opportunities and of access to training and educational programmes – but what happens if the access damages the right of another's access?

Should the learner have equal opportunities for success in training and educational programmes?

The answers are difficult. If the reasons for a failure to succeed can be clearly placed on the wilful neglect of set work by a student then that student has no right to be passed by the examiner. The difficulty lies in failure due to an inequality of opportunity before the learner embarked on the programme. Again, this issue will be discussed later on but a tentative right can be suggested at this stage.

The right of learners to succeed at a learning programme provided that they carry out the required study and coursework.

================= **ACTIVITY** =================

Selecting and restating your list of learner's rights.
In this activity I would like you to make a list of your own student's or trainee's rights. Read the following list of suggested learner's rights which have been presented in this chapter and select those which you think are important. You may need to rewrite each statement to suit your own training or educational situations.

- the learner's right to know the truth
- the right to expect that the trainer or the teacher is *an authority* in their particular subject area
- the right to expect us to know about the regulations and procedures which will end in the successful completion of the programme
- the right to expect to achieve independence in learning
- the right of the learner to expect the teacher to work in the learner's best long-term interests as far as these interests are agreed and understood
- the right to expect to be treated with respect
- the right to special training and education for the learner who has naturally inherited and educationally important advantages or disadvantages
- the right to equal opportunities in access to training and educational programmes
- the right of the learner to succeed at a learning programme provided that he or she carries out the required study and coursework.

THE CHARTERS FOR FURTHER AND HIGHER EDUCATION

In 1994 the British government issued a Charter for Higher Education to cover all universities and colleges offering full- or part-time courses or other programmes of study. This Charter applies to England (there are other Charters for Scotland and Wales). The Higher Education Charter covers a level beyond GCE A-level and its vocational equivalent. There is also a Further Education Charter which covers non-advanced further education.

The Charter for Higher Education is an attempt by the Department for Education to set out the rights of learners. This quotation is from the beginning of the Charter:

> ...everyone has the right to expect good service
> from higher education. Better information
> and improved choice will help everyone make
> the most of what universities and colleges offer.

Here is a summary of what is covered in the charter:

● Clear and accurate information about:
  – universities and colleges and the courses they offer
  – the usual entry requirements
  – the quality of what they provide
  – the residential accommodation available
  – facilities for people with disabilities or learning difficulties.
● Fair and efficient handling of your application.
● Full and accurate information about the financial help available.
● Your university or college will:
  – explain the aims and structure of courses
  – allow students to register their views about the courses
  – give a high standard of teaching, guidance and counselling
  – ensure proper arrangements for student security and safety.
● At all times students are entitled to equal treatment regardless of sex or ethnic background.

The Charter for Further and Adult Education contains similar declarations but there is a greater emphasis on careers guidance.

The Charter covers many of the theoretical rights discussed in this chapter. It is interesting that there is also a note for learners about their responsibilities:

To get the most out of teaching and learning, students themselves have certain responsibilities. For example, they should take part in seminars, attend lectures and practicals on time and hand in work promptly. Some universities and colleges are setting out the responsibilities of institutions and students in 'learner agreements'....

Chapter 5

Prejudice and Equal Opportunities

CONCEPTS

Prejudice
Causes of prejudice
Reducing prejudice
Equality in learning
Sex
Age
Ethnic origin
Belief
Physical barriers
Mental barriers

PREJUDICE

As I sit down to write this chapter I know that it is almost impossible to discuss this topic without someone taking offence.

Some years ago I had a Jewish colleague who had escaped as a teenager from Germany in 1938. At the beginning of the war she said she was furious with the British authorities because she had been forcibly turned away from 'getting at' some people of German descent who were being interned. 'Fascists' she called the British who had stopped her. Even in the early 1960s she would still not admit that the internees had the same rights under British law as she had claimed in her escape to this country.

What is it that turns factual description into racism? I have just said that my colleague was Jewish and that the internees were German. There is nothing inaccurate or prejudiced about either statement. One person came from a well-established Jewish family and the others were born and had lived in Germany for many years. It is when you add a value judgement to the words – like applying 'Fascist' to the British authorities – that the interpretation turns from one of simple description to prejudice.

Let me try to be safe, using myself and my brother as an example. I will try to discuss the topic without giving offence but examples are necessary for the explanation of any principle! I am labouring the point to show that one of the main difficulties to the resolution of prejudice is that everyone is so defensive. My brother and I have red hair. Everyone knows that all red-headed people have bad tempers, don't they? As it happens my brother and I are fairly easy going. We have our faults but a raggy temper is not one of them. We, as individuals who are not bad tempered, can do nothing about the general view that red-heads have a bad temper. This is the nature of prejudice. It is a belief which is held as a general view by a group of people and this belief is held even though the evidence may be totally contradictory.

⇨   **STOP AND REFLECT**   ⇦

Are you free from all prejudices?
What are the main causes of prejudice?

CAUSES OF PREJUDICE

Prejudice is so widespread in human relationships that you can probably think of many examples; here are three suggestions of causes:

- historical/traditional
- stereotyping
- scapegoating.

Historical/traditional

It is quite amazing how long many historical and traditional disputes have been running. The start of the divisions may have been long before any possible living memory and the circumstances may have changed completely and the connection with the original trouble may be very tenuous indeed. People seem take sides and they love those in their 'team' and love to hate those on the opposite side. Often it is a sign of maturity when the next generation is fully inducted into the hatred and prejudice.

Once I was chatting to a woman from Ethiopia and discussing the traditional view of the Wise Men in the Bible. One of these kings is usually illustrated as being a black-skinned man. We agreed that he would probably have been seen as coming from the Horn of Africa. She told me that the land disputes in that area go back for hundreds if not thousands of years. Her own family were in a dispute over land which could be traced back for 900 years. She said some pretty rude things about the family on the other side of the land dispute and I said that it sounded rather like the traditional dispute between Yorkshire and Lancashire. Some Northerners believe that the prejudice between Yorkshire and Lancashire has its roots in the Wars of the Roses but such a link is most unlikely to be correct. However, this doesn't prevent fierce rivalry at cricket matches and blaming the antagonism on events which took place in the fourteenth century!

Many prejudices with a basis in ancient disputes are handed down from generation to generation, by father to son and mother to daughter so that involvement in the 'cause' becomes a mark of belonging. Sometimes the prejudice seems harmless but other times it is not. 'Trelawney's army', all dressed in black and gold, are regarded as harmless and rather charming as they march to Twickenham when Cornwall reaches the Rugby Union County finals. The real trouble with traditional prejudice comes when it has the backing and respectability of traditional authority; 'Jingoism' and 'nationalism' are very powerful forces.

ACTIVITY

Looking for historical roots as a basis of prejudice.
Select a dispute with which you are familiar and ask yourself, 'How long has this been going on?' You may well find that the roots of the dispute go back a very long way. Ask yourself if you were there when the original dispute began or if you have heard about the dispute from older people. Does it have roots before the experience of people you know? Now, try to write an explanation of the dispute for your own students.

Stereotyping

Regarding my example about red-headed people, I think I can understand why people with red hair gained a reputation for quick temper. I once caught sight of myself in the mirror when I was in a rare rage. It was an astonishing sight. My face was dead white and a violent 'V' birthmark was enflamed on my forehead. My red hair seemed to be standing on end like waving orange tentacles. I had to laugh and, of course, my rage subsided. If red-headed people look so impressively annoyed then it is no wonder that the impression sticks in other people's mind. Sometimes there is a basis for stereotyping as a general use because it is simply easier. As with perception, we become lazy about working out what we are seeing each time. We tend to have a quick glimpse and then say, 'Hello, another one of those', without looking to make quite certain that we really did see what we assumed we saw.

This habit of jumping quickly to a conclusion saves time in everyday living. I do not have to check in detail that it really is my husband upstairs with me in our house every day. A small cough or a tread on the floorboard is characteristic enough for identification. This useful short circuit to avoid full thought and analysis is the most difficult barrier to realizing when a useful habit has turned into stereotyping. Nothing I can do will rid my father, husband and two sons of the belief that they are 'helping' me with the housework. I am meant to be grateful for their occasional assistance with what they clearly regard as my sole responsibility and to not expect them to share the housework regularly as a matter of course. The implication behind this attitude is the stereotype of 'woman's work'.

ACTIVITY

Do you stereotype?
This is a very difficult activity because most of us feel that we are free from prejudice, but I would like you to write a list of all those people that we tend to 'ignore' or 'lump together'. Usually this list of people includes those beyond our personal experience but you may find that there are some with whom you do have day-to-day contact.

Scapegoating

My mother once caused a minor sensation in the local post office by telling the postmaster that she needed another stamp because she had licked all the gum off the one he had just sold her. He immediately went into a tirade about it being the first time that anyone to his knowledge had ever licked off all the gum. Amid general laughter the postmaster gave my mother a new stamp and then they discussed how everyone always seemed to want to blame someone or something else rather than their own actions.

Most societies have majority and minority groups. Every country seems to have a minority group which takes the brunt of the 'aren't they stupid' jokes. It is interesting to see how the nationality of the group changes from country to country. The jokes do not seem to vary. This is a clear case of scapegoating. The majority need someone else to blame when things go wrong. Any convenient minority group will do for this purpose, especially if there is a traditional feud between the two groups in the first place.

Scapegoating can become very serious when outside events put pressure on the whole society. If natural disaster or an economic slump affect a group then one of the first reactions is to find some smaller group to blame. It is one of the mechanisms by which minority groups get victimized and that border disputes begin. As every dictator knows, the best way to settle unrest within a community is to start a war with a neighbour so that there is someone else to blame for our home-brewed ills.

ACTIVITY

Identify when you make other people a scapegoat.
Again, this is another activity which is hard to do because blaming other people is such a comfortable thing to do in everyday life. I find it fascinating to watch other people who, when they have made a mistake, blame everything and everybody else – but it is extremely difficult to recognize this tendency in oneself! Make a list of the last lot of 'blames' that you have put on other people and other things and then ask yourself if they were really the cause or if you might, yourself, have been a little bit responsible.

REDUCING PREJUDICE

Here are three means by which prejudice might be reduced:

- legislation
- familiarity
- group success.

Legislation

There has been some opposition to the Race Relations Act and the Equal Opportunities Act in the UK. In writing these books I have been struggling with the dilemma of 'his and her' and trying to talk about prejudice without offending any particular group of readers. In practice the 'his and her' problem is a menace because it ruins the flow of English language and pushes the gender issue to the exclusion of all others, but in theory I approve. How else are women ever going to make a dent on traditional male attitudes? Legislation does give strength to argue against entrenched traditional or historical prejudices.

According to the sociologist Weber, there are three bases of authority:

- traditional – authority based on elders, kings, fathers, etc.
- legal-rational – authority based on the law of the land
- charismatic – authority based on the personality of a popular leader.

Leaders such as Martin Luther King tried to use their charismatic authority to reduce traditional prejudice and some of these personal crusades were very effective. However, it is by pitting the legal-rational authority of the law of the land against traditional prejudice that most progress can be made.

There is an expression which I use to highlight an attack on historical and traditional prejudices:

Truth has nothing to do with being in the majority.

This is an anti-democratic statement. It means that a majority can be wrong; in many traditional prejudices the majority *are* wrong. For this reason I support the use of the law in trying to reduce historical and traditional prejudice.

⇨ **STOP AND REFLECT** ⇦

Do you think that legislation can be a forceful way to change prejudice?

If not, what other ways would you use to attack deep-seated prejudice?

Familiarity

When I was younger I could not stand the Welsh. This childhood prejudice stemmed from a few trips into north Wales from the north of England. There is traditional hostility between these two areas. I found that if I talked with a Scottish accent any hostility disappeared and I got an earful about the horrid English. Later I realized that our new nextdoor-neighbour was a very 'Welsh' Welshman called Mr Thomas. You could not meet a nicer, kinder person and a better neighbour. Now I was in a difficulty. I knew I could not stand Welshmen but I really liked Mr Thomas. Something had to give on one side or the other. In practice it was much easier to drop the prejudice about the Welsh than to deny that Mr Thomas was very nice.

This story illustrates how very easily familiarity with and knowledge of other people can be a sure way of reducing prejudice. I don't mean that you should love everyone indiscriminately; unquestioning affection is just as prejudiced as unthinking animosity. I have a way of detecting whether I have general prejudice against any particular group in our society: if I can think of a person from that group whom I heartily dislike and another person from the same group whom I really like then I know that I am discriminating between people, not stereotyping the group as a whole.

ACTIVITY

Reconsidering your prejudices.
Make a list of the people who have helped you, or whom you quite like, who belong to groups which you do not usually find very helpful. You may have to root about a bit to find examples but everyday contact in shopping or travel may give you some examples. When you have isolated one or two cases, ask youself why you are surprised that you had a good feeling rather than the expected bad feeling.

Group success

Years ago at my college we finished the first term of teacher training with a team teaching exercise and my particular presentation was on the general theme of survival. Several years later, when I was on a teacher exchange in Australia, I met a fellow member of my team. How great it was to see each other again! What a time we had gossiping and reminiscing about our shared experience! Most of it, I suspect, was pure imagination but the feeling of goodwill was very real indeed. Shared experience has a powerful binding effect on team members, especially if the group experience is successful.

When people work together on an equal footing, especially if the task is demanding and interesting, the barriers which separate off minority groups tend to disappear. Team work, using mixed groups, is a very effective way of learning to overcome the separation of people into hostile groups. It is a way of uniting people rather than dividing them on the basis of their origins.

ACTIVITY

Group experience to reduce prejudice.
Consider a learning group in which there may be underlying prejudice. Can you think of a learning activity

which will bind the group together through challenge and mutual, successful experience?

EQUALITY IN LEARNING

It is interesting that the Further Education Charter recently published by the Department for Education concentrates very much on careers guidance, as this extract shows:

> If you are thinking about education and training options – full-time or part-time, and whatever your age – you can get initial information and advice from Careers Offices. Employers can also get information on education and training in their area from the Training and Enterprise Council.

This is putting emphasis on the need for full information on what is available so that the right to equal opportunities in education can work in practice. The government, validating bodies, universities, colleges and all educational establishments seem to have a stated equal opportunities policy and most appear to be paying more than lip-service to the principle. This is from my own university's policy:

> The aim of this policy is to ensure that no job applicant, student or employee receives less favourable treatment on the grounds of sex, age, race, colour, nationality, ethnic or national origins, marital status, sexual orientation, family responsibility, trade union activity, disability, political or religious belief.

I am quite sure that the university takes this policy very seriously and everything is done to make certain that access to learning is as open as possible. Also, the administrators and the lecturers try as far as possible to ensure that the learners are successful at the end of the course, provided that they work and study hard.

⇒   **STOP AND REFLECT**   ⇐

In the last chapter we considered general learners' rights. Now think about the following statements and consider the justification for calling them 'rights':

- the right to special training and education for every student who has naturally inherited and educationally important advantages or disadvantages
- the right to equal opportunities in access to training and educational programmes
- the right to succeed at a learning programme provided that the required study and coursework has been carried out.

Specific areas of equal opportunity policy in education and training will be looked at in more detail in the rest of this chapter. Key points are likely to turn on three questions:

- Is there a functional difference between the group and the general population?
- Is there access to education?
- Is the expectation of successful study a reality?

SEX

There is an under-representation of women in such areas as science, engineering and technology. As the only girl among 16 boys in the science sixth-form at school, I have had first-hand experience of this. Some researchers have suggested that there is evidence that the brain development within the female foetus may be slightly different from the development of the brain within the male foetus.

The root of gender stereotyping lies in early childhood. Primary school teachers have noted for years that little girls seem to learn to read more quickly than little boys. Teachers seem to be resigned to working hard to drag boys into literacy. Nobody seems to have thought about spending as much effort to drag the majority of little girls into mechanical and spatial reasoning. Such inequalities could be dealt with by remedial science for girls early in school teaching but, at present, teachers and trainers of women usually have to struggle with a poor knowledge base.

I used to teach science to caterers, hairdressers and pre-nursing courses. Much of the time I started with learners who were not neutral. They were damaged and shell-shocked by their miserable failures at science in school. It was difficult to restore their confidence and gain their trust but when we started to take stock we found that they knew a great deal. Examples of the basic principles of science are littered about the kitchen, the hairdressing salon and the human body. School science had concentrated on 'boy mechanic' examples which did not mean anything to non-mechanical boys and most of the girls. I call this a functional inequality and a disadvantage.

The problem of a male bias in the teaching of science can be remedied by better teacher training and an emphasis on more and improved science for everyone in the primary schools. I have great hopes for the use of the splendid developments in information technology and multi-media packs in creating exciting and effective science teaching materials for all learners.

ACTIVITY

Taking a balanced view of sex bias in education.
It is very difficult not to be partisan in the area of sexual discrimination, especially in education. In this activity try, in your imagination, to swap over to the other sex and ask yourself to list the bias you might experience. Role-reversal is a good way of coming to understand another person's point of view.

AGE

There is clear evidence of functional differences in learning between the young and the old. It is said that no mathematician has ever had an original mathematical inspiration after the age of 25. Mathematicians can go on producing variations on a theme into old age but truly creative and original mathematical ideas fade at a remarkably early age. The facility which seems to fade is the mental agility, the working memory.

There is one important caveat to this statement. When someone learnt a skill in youth and continues to practise that skill then there is no falling away with age. My father started his working life in a Scottish bank and one of his earliest jobs was to total ledger pages in pounds, shillings and pence. He became so adept at this that he could run his finger down the page and add up as he went along. He could write in the accurate total at the bottom of the page without writing down any intermediary figures. This skill stayed with him in extreme old age so that he used to delight in totting up my supermarket receipts, just to check that the machine was working properly.

I think that there is a functional difference in the confidence of older learners. This seems to work both ways and is two sides of the same factor. On the one hand, there is a strong tendency not to admit that there is any need for learning at all – the 'Don't teach your Grandmother to suck eggs' syndrome. On the other hand, this rigidity seems to mask the underlying lack of confidence and security which makes an older learner fear that success at learning is not possible at an older age. Older people can learn new skills but it may take a little longer than it would have done in earlier days. The main barrier to learning can be self-doubt.

There is widespread, and unjustified, discrimination against older workers in recruiting for jobs which involve acquiring new skills. It may be quicker to retrain older learners than it is to train young people, but many people over 50 are treated as unemployable even though they possess excellent mental and physical skills.

━━━━━━━━ **ACTIVITY** ━━━━━━━━

Consider your own old age.
List the things that you think you will resent being told how to do by younger people when you get old.

ETHNIC ORIGIN

I have taught overseas, I have taught overseas students in the UK and I have taught students from ethnic minorities within the UK. Come to think of it, I have taught ethnic minorities overseas as well! There are differences in each of these situations.

The first thing that I realized when teaching overseas is that the British education system is only one of many. Education systems are very specific to the country of origin. Principles which apply in the UK may be unacceptable or completely strange in another country. For example, here we accept the idea that teachers should be self-aware so that they can empathize with the learner, but in India the principle of 'self-awareness' is part of a mystical concept completely divorced from education. There are difficulties at every stage. I felt very disadvantaged in the classroom because I could not read the pupils' non-verbal communication. Equally, the differences in fundamental educational systems and methods can create inequality for anyone entering our learning system from another country.

Overseas students in this country usually come from a majority culture at home and they are often gifted or privileged learners within their own society. Because of these factors they expect to be able to retain many of their existing learning and study habits. It seems a shame that so much time is often wasted in learning new study methods rather than really essential skills and knowledge. Fortunately many do not have to learn a new language as well.

It is fortunate for overseas students in the UK that English is spoken so widely throughout the world. Though current English usage may be a barrier to learning for a short time, and we should be aware of this difficulty with overseas students, it is nothing like as difficult as it is for overseas students in, say, Germany, where I saw almost all the overseas students having to learn German before they could even start to learn the subject matter.

The inequalities suffered by ethnic minorities in the UK relate to the degree of integration into the wider society. Some learners who come from very closed communities in Britain may have disadvantages which are as severe as for any person newly arrived from overseas and from a totally different culture. For example, I have taught women in the London Borough of Tower Hamlets who had exactly the same problems of understanding English, teaching methods and subject matter as the women I taught in a class in Calcutta. On the other hand, some learners of minority ethnic origin are second or third generation British born and completely familiar with the language, methods and basic principles.

⇨ **STOP AND REFLECT** ⇦

Many countries have benefited from the presence of people from other cultures. How much integration is needed before the benefits can be experienced by the host society?

Do you think that newcomers to a society should learn and use the language and customs of the host society?

Do you think that groups of people from other countries should hold onto their language, customs and life-style so that they form a discrete minority culture within the host community?

BELIEF

Many of the arguments about religious discrimination lie not in equal opportunities, access to education nor success in study by hard work but in conflict over what is being taught. These questions turn out to be ones of ethical relativity. The debate turns on which ethic takes precedence in an educational context.

Suppose that one religious group decrees that the Bible has to be taken literally. This means that the Creation is believed as written and the theories of evolution and the works of Charles Darwin are rejected. Suppose that we are fundamental believers in Islam: we believe every word of the Koran and this belief casts doubts on the way in which equal opportunities for women are interpreted in the UK.

George Steiner in his lecture 'Has truth a future?'(1978) suggested dogma and mysticism were two of the four main enemies of scientific truth. It may be difficult to defend the British system of an established church, the crown and parliamentary democracy but the system does give some protection against the extremes of dogma and mysticism.

⇨   **STOP AND REFLECT**   ⇦

All education systems have an underpinning religious, moral and social basis because the prime objective is to initiate the young into the existing system – for right or wrong! Here are some questions which you might like to consider about the fundamental basis for a national educational system:

- Should a religious belief prevent anyone from taking a full part in the available learning process?
- Should belief interfere with the search for scientific truth?
- Should a minority group's belief alter the traditional British right of free speech and freedom for the individual?

PHYSICAL BARRIERS

Many years ago there was a welder who wanted to work in a primary school which catered for children with physical disabilities. He was creative and imaginative and he wanted to weld metal supports for individual children so that they could get into a comfortable position to take full part in the learning activities, but he was not allowed to do this. He wasn't a qualified primary teacher, so he could not become a full-time member of staff at the school. Several college lecturers, a kind headmaster of a secondary school and a few officials bent the rules a bit so that he could practise what he wanted to do. I think of this cheerful person whenever the subject of physical barriers to learning comes up.

⇨ **STOP AND REFLECT** ⇦

How do you approach people who have physical barriers to learning?

Do you shout at those who are profoundly deaf?

Do you know how to guide someone who has severe visual barriers?

Have you considered how difficult it is to get into your building if you have to go by wheelchair?

MENTAL BARRIERS

When a teacher appreciates the vast capacity of the human brain, he or she will realize that the inability to learn can be placed at the door of the teacher rather than the learner. All teachers should be prepared to accept that the range of normal human behaviour is very wide indeed and if teachers have any doubt – look at other teachers! I think that if a learner has genuine brain function and personality disorder barriers to learning, the best interests of the learner are served by those who are trained in this area. I do not think that the normal classroom teacher or trainer can do justice to a student with mental barriers to learning in a group of students; this work belongs properly to trained experts in the field.

Chapter 6

Attitudes and Assertiveness

 CONCEPTS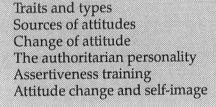

Traits and types
Sources of attitudes
Change of attitude
The authoritarian personality
Assertiveness training
Attitude change and self-image

TRAITS AND TYPES

The family photographs of my mother range from pictures of a little girl of 2 to pictures of an 80-year-old just before she died. In every picture throughout her student days, early motherhood and sporting grandmotherhood she remains clearly the same person. Some psychologists rely on this constancy to test individuals for persistent personality traits rather like an analytical chemist tries to find out the chemical composition of a mixture. Other psychologists defend the ability of individuals to control their own development and growth and to change their personality.

89

⇨ **STOP AND REFLECT** ⇦

Do you think that your personality has been determined already?

Do you think you can change it at will (if you want to change)?

I am unwilling to accept that everything has been determined and set beforehand. My favourite psychological theory was proposed by George Kelly (1955) who said: 'You are not a victim of your own biography'.

Everyone starts off with a set genetic makeup which comes from our biological parents and an outside chance of a little individual variation. Everyone undergoes experiences which influence their development but no one's personality is totally predetermined. George Kelly describes this mixture of nature and nurture as the individual person acting like a scientist who tests the incoming information and then decides whether or not to alter the usual response. Kelly describes an independent person who can cope with any change but who operates from a steady platform built on natural inheritance and experience.

Personality theorists may put forward a simple model and suggest one or two fundamental characteristics which are the main reasons for a person's behaviour. These theorists are looking for a general type. Eysenck (1981) proposed the extravert-introvert and stable-neurotic dimensions as characteristics of the normal person. Some psychologists believe that bodily functions are the main influence on human behaviour and that these form the control and basis for action. All sorts of amazing theories have been put forward, from lumps on the head to body shape. These types of theories go back to the ancient Greeks who defined:

● endomorphs – easy-going people
● mesomorphs – muscular and fit people
● ectomorphs – skinny, nervous and intellectual people.

Others, like Guildford (1954), suggest a complex of many interrelated traits to account for our actions. Like a careful artist painting an intricate picture, Guildford identified 180 different aspects of personality. When you study this work on personality traits even 180 differences do not seem to be enough. Individual people are capable of infinite variety.

I am going to concentrate on one aspect of personality which is described by both the trait and type theorists. This is the balance between aggression and submission. Personal change is essential in education and training and a learner cannot change if he or she is too aggressive or too submissive. If we assume that George Kelly was right and that we are all capable of change then the most effective behaviour will come from a clear-headed, realistic determination which is balanced between aggression and submission.

SOURCES OF ATTITUDES

Apart from the individual genes which we inherit, attitudes are influenced by everything which happens to us.

ACTIVITY

Reflecting on your own experience.
This is a long list of the sort of experiences you may have had which affected your own attitudes; as you read through the list try to reflect on what influence the various experiences may have had. This reflection should help you to understand your own attitudes, and if you take your time over this activity you should become better able to reflect on your students' attitudes.

Country of origin	Childhood spent in town or rural area
Childhood economically buoyant	Childhood economically depressed
Mother's occupation	Father's occupation
Number of brothers	Number of sisters

Most significant other relation	Significant adults in childhood
Home size and comfort	Access to parks and recreations
Holidays and travel	Diet, cooking, drinking at home
Books and access to information technology	Television,videos,tapes, radio
Arts, theatre, cinema	Sports and hobbies
Religion and belief	Clubs and social links
School and college	Job and workmates
Peers	Friends

⇨　**STOP AND REFLECT**　⇦

This has been a long activity so it is probably a good time to think about what you decided. Try the following questions:

Which were the most important influences on your attitudes?

Do you have a wide spread of influence or does influence come down to just one or two things?

There are values within our society which influence our basis for action:

- *Formal* – these directions come from official authorities; the basis for such principles in this country is Christian ethics – *rules, laws and policies*.
- *Societal* – these directions come from within society which is the basis of a particular culture – *group norms*.
- *Personal* – these directions come from within the individual person. They are the result of working memory and thinking – 'What I think is right'.

CHANGE OF ATTITUDE

'The way to hell is paved with good intentions'. This old quotation sums up the difficulty that people find in making real changes.

A simple change which is attempted by many people is losing weight. Changes which are doomed to failure in most cases include:

- spending a fortune on 'slimming foods'
- starving for a few days
- taking up an unusual diet, such as only eating bananas
- making the whole family change their eating habits too
- taking up unusual exercises.

These changes fail because they are difficult to maintain over a long period of time. You may not have enough money for specialist foods, the family may rebel, you may start bingeing, and jogging can be a serious hazard to health for the middle-aged!

The secret of permanent change is:

- *Compatibility with life style,* eg, in slimming this may be rescheduling meals in the day or taking up gentle exercise which is pleasurable and fun
- *Linked to self-image and self-esteem*, eg, in slimming this may be thinking of yourself as a thin person and aiming to fit into those nice, smaller clothes in the wardrobe.

ACTIVITY

Try a change of attitude.
You might regard this activity as a test of your ability to have a closed mind! Think of something or some principle upon which you hold very firm views. Write down a list of arguments which could be used against this principle. I do not want to encourage you into a total state of indecision but I do want you to consider how long ago it was that you saw another person's point of view.

Resistance to attitude change

Extremeness – some people hold very extreme views and have to make a much greater effort if they are to achieve change. Many people holding extreme views did not reach their position by learning in a voluntary way but have undergone a process of indoctrination. The process of conversion or indoctrination often seems to involve physical hardship and a sudden and violent 'seeing the light' experience.

Multiplicity – attitudes are often enmeshed in a range of other attitudes. When I pull out one attitude to see if I want to change it, I pull out a whole lot more. It is rather like trying to pull a chunk of pond-weed out of a garden pool.

Consistency – sometimes there is an intellectual resistance to change. I have worked out a logical reason for a particular attitude and I may be reluctant to rethink the logic of that attitude.

THE AUTHORITARIAN PERSONALITY

A lot of current discussion moves around the idea of the fixed authoritarian personality and both aggression and submission are linked to authoritarianism. One of the important aspects of personal effectiveness in learning, as well as in other aspects of life, is getting the balance between aggression and submission right. This correct balance is the basis of assertiveness training and the subsequent change in attitude, so it may be helpful to look at some early work in the area.

I find work on the authoritarian personality carried out in the late 1940s particularly interesting because it is a clear example of how historical events can influence research. Adorno (1947) and his fellow workers were investigating the subject just at the end of the Second World War. At that time the full horrors of the Nazi holocaust were being revealed and I remember the first pictures of Belsen on the newsreels. There was a strong desire to stamp out Fascism for ever and I think that Adorno blamed the authoritarian personality for what had happened. The Fascist or 'f-scale' of measurement for authoritarian attitudes is still influential today.

Here are some notes on Adorno's theory with statements which indicate authoritarian attitudes.

Authoritarian aggression

The tendency to look for and condemn, reject and punish people who violate conventional values.

> Sex crimes, such as rape and attacks on children, deserve more than mere imprisonment; such criminals ought to be publicly whipped or worse.

Authoritarian submission

Uncritical attitude towards idealized moral authorities of the in-group.

> What this country needs most, more than laws and political programmes, is a few courageous, tireless, devoted leaders in whom the people can put their trust.

Superstition and stereotyping

Belief in mystical determinants of the individual's fate; the disposition to think in rigid categories.

> Science has its place but there are many important things that can never possibly be understood by the human mind.

Power and toughness

Preoccupation with the dominance:weakness, strong:weak, leader:follower dimension and identification with power figures; exaggerated assertion of strength and toughness.

> No weakness or difficulty can hold us back if we have enough will power.

Destructiveness and cynicism

Generalized hostility and vilification of human beings.

Human nature being what it is, there will always be war and conflict.

Projectivity

Belief in unconscious influences.

Most people don't realize how much of our lives are controlled by plots hatched in secret places.

These factors are clearly aimed at the extremists of the time. However, George Steiner (1978) had another 'enemy of scientific truth', which was relative truth. He referred to Marxism and communism as examples of influences which distorted the pursuit of truth.

⇨ **STOP AND REFLECT** ⇦

What is your opinion of Adorno's theory?
  Do you think that Adorno's list of attitudes for the authoritarian personality can apply to all extremists?
  Do you think that a person who holds an attitude by reason of indoctrination has basic characteristics which are suggested by the examples taken from the f-scale?

ASSERTIVENESS TRAINING

Learning in general and learning to change attitudes in particular depend on getting the balance between aggression and submission right. This is the basis of assertiveness training.

═══════════════ **ACTIVITY** ═══════════════

Discovering your assertiveness.
Tape record a sample of your own conversation and then analyse the content according to the categories: submissive, aggressive and assertive.

Find out which dominates your conversation by looking for instances of the following:

> long rambling statements
> self-justifications
> statements beginning with, 'It's only my opinion...', 'Would you mind...', 'Sorry, but...', or 'Er....' followed by a long pause
> – *mark these 'submissive'*
>
> excessive use of 'I'
> blank expressions like 'Rubbish' and 'That won't work'
> threats like 'You'd better not do...'
> putting people down
> 'ought', 'must', 'should'
> blaming others
> – *mark these 'aggressive'*
>
> brief statements
> clear statements beginning with 'I'
> distinguishing between fact and opinion
> open-ended questions
> resolving conflicts and problems
> questioning what lies behind propositions
> – *mark these 'assertive'.*

An assertive person is not over-aggressive or over-submissive but handles everyday situations well. To assert means to state: positively, assuredly, plainly, strongly.

According to a book called *Don't Say 'YES' When You Want to Say 'NO'* (Fensterheim, 1976) there are four characteristics of assertive people; they:

● reveal their real selves in words and actions
● have an active orientation to life
● act in a way which brings self-respect
● communicate with other people at all levels.

Assertiveness training begins by identifying particular assertiveness problems such as those discussed here.

The timid soul

This type of person is constantly placating other people because they fear that they may have offended them. They have difficulty in expressing their legitimate wishes and are constantly manoeuvered into a position which they do not like. They tend to be easily hurt and feel self-conscious when with people in authority. They are often lonely and get pushed around because other people's wishes seem to be more important.

The person with communications problems

These people seem to be very verbose and disguise their ideas with trivia. They are often dishonest about their real feelings and attitudes because they fear that they may reveal some attitude which could be criticized. Their difficulty lies mostly in poor social skills and inadequate interpersonal perceptions.

A 'split' assertive who has confident and timid responses

Some people have confident and perceptive areas of their lives but have 'blind' spots where they fail to cope with the situation. An example of this would be where an individual is very successful at work but a social duffer at personal relationships.

People with other behavioural defects

Many types of behaviour give the wrong impression or indicate an inability to cope. Here are some examples:

inability to maintain eye contact
confusing aggression with assertiveness
treating every stranger as if they were a friend
expecting reasonableness from others
feeling that other people owe you a living
living vicariously through your children.

Assertiveness training schemes identify the individual problem, work out an action plan, set reasonable and achievable objectives and plan for another person to monitor progress. Generally there are three areas of learning which help the change to a balanced approach:

- *Principles* – getting the balance right so that you have respect for yourself and respect for others without aggression, intimidation or being patronizing.
- *Speech* – positive and specific, and avoiding being negative or vague.
- *Body* – calm breathing, relaxed posture and a confident manner.

ATTITUDE CHANGE AND SELF-IMAGE

The most damaging effect of inequality is the 'looking-glass effect' of other people's attitudes on an individual's self-esteem and self-image. If a woman, for example, is constantly being regarded, along with other women, as a second-class person, then this continuous denigration has an effect on the way in which she sees herself. It can happen in such subtle ways. Think of the difference in meaning of the following terms:

master – mistress
a dog – a bitch
old boy – old girl

There are two ways in which a change of attitude can help to improve an individual's self-image. First, general attitudes within the population can be addressed in the ways which were described in Chapter 5 on reducing prejudice and second, assertiveness training can be used to induce an internal and personal change.

ACTIVITY

An assertiveness exercise.

List some recent occasions when you feel that you were at a disadvantage or you feel that, in retrospect, you could have done better.

Pick one of these events that you would like to improve.

Make a list of why your behaviour was inadequate.

List the people, events, situations and circumstances which you feel made successful behaviour difficult.

Day-dream about the situation, events and circumstances which you might wish had happened and then turn these day-dreams into a practical scenario.

Plan how you can bring together an event at which you can have a second attempt at getting things right. Check all details to make sure that you are not over-confident and make plans for how you are going to cope if events turn out differently.

Do not put this plan into effect because you are very likely to fall flat on your face again! But do use the positive planning and ideas for the next event when you are unsure of what to do.

Chapter 7

Emotions, Affective Learning and Intrapersonal Skills

KNOWING ONESELF – CONTENTS OR CHARACTERISTICS?

To study life in plants and animals (including humans) we have to understand the organic chemistry of reactions in living cells. For a long time there was a paradox in this basic work: to study life, first the plant or the animal had to be killed. Later on, biologists found that they had missed many of the essential chemical pathways because these pathways ceased to exist when the plant or animal cells were dead. Research had to switch to the study of living things. There are two ways of analysing how living things function:

- Content – where the whole is broken into smaller parts to work out how it is made.
- Characteristics – where the whole system is studied to see the characteristic operations.

In the same way we must be careful when we are attempting to learn about ourselves. It can be very damaging to try to break down our personality and to become over analytical because we may destroy the delicate balance of our own unique self. It is much better to take the 'characteristic' approach and thoroughly learn how we operate in everyday life.

I believe that people are happier and more effective when they understand their own strengths and weaknesses. If we understand our own feelings and emotions and the way our own mind works then we have more space and time to get on with the really interesting task of understanding and interacting with other people. There is one important condition to this self-awareness: it must be a process of understanding our own characteristics and not a self-destructive breakdown of our own parts and contents. We could seriously damage our whole personality by such a drastic process!

EMOTIONS

Let us have another look at the six primary emotions universally accepted and recognized by people all over the world no matter what language they speak or what culture or race they belong to:

- surprise
- disgust
- fear
- anger
- happiness
- sadness.

Recent experiments have shown some remarkable findings. Unlike most non-verbal communication, which is highly culture-bound and most confusing to the foreigner, the facial expressions for these six emotions are universally understood. Japanese culture requires certain facial expressions to be adopted in certain situations and this convention is commonly observed. When a Japanese audience was secretly filmed as they watched sad, funny, frightening or digusting films their facial expressions were easily understood by people of widely different cultural backgrounds.

There are three components of any emotion:

- *Internal perception* – our internal emotion depends entirely upon our own point of view. We may regard a lion with joy as a likeable, flat-faced, soft, furry thing or with fear as a ferocious beast.
- *Body changes* – there is a balance between the sympathetic (excitatory) and the parasympathetic (normalizing) nervous sytem. In addition, the endocrine system pumps body hormones into our blood stream so that the two systems, nervous and hormonal, produce physical effects such as slowing down heart rate or 'butterflies in the stomach'.
- *Resulting behaviour* – this is the way we react to the prompting of our mind and body. Major individual differences occur here. One person may be frozen with fear and another may move smoothly into well-trained coping strategies.

Although there is almost nothing we can do about body changes, we can learn coping strategies. Men and women employed in the emergency services have all been trained to produce effective behaviour when they are faced with highly emotional situations. Counsellors and health professionals are trained to help other people to learn coping skills for personal distress.

We can learn to increase our personal effectiveness if we learn to cope with our own emotions. This does not mean pretending that we don't have emotions but learning how to express appropriate emotions. The first skill is to recognize a true emotional response and to be able to identify 'faked' emotions.

⇨ **STOP AND REFLECT** ⇦

How do you tell if someone is telling lies?
How do you work out if someone is trying to display fake emotions?

The main cue is to watch for a match between bodily reaction and the verbal communication. Fear, represented by a paler face, sweat and anxious glances, is easy to identify even if the person is speaking bold words. There are rituals of body language which are often easy to interpret within a particular culture. In British society, liars often cover their mouths as they speak.

Non-verbal communication and emotions

Many sales and business management programmes try to teach non-verbal signals which go with certain emotional responses. 'Smile when you answer the telephone' is the advice given to telephone sale trainees. 'Always raise the pitch of your voice at the end of a phrase or sentence' is good advice for actors in comedy productions. Both these behaviours indicate joy.

There are complex cultural differences in behaviour. In British society you are not believed if you don't look the other person in the eye when talking or listening. Yet in some cultures a woman looking a man in the eye is regarded as too bold and such behaviour is unacceptable. By contrast, there is a native American saying, 'Eyes should meet when men talk'. It is very easy to offend when we are not aware of the 'local' non-verbal rules. I find myself at a severe disadvantage when I teach overseas because I cannot interpret the non-verbal signals. Personal space, which was covered in Chapter 2, can also be critical in such situations because I can make other people feel threatened or give out hostile non-verbal signals unconsciously when someone else gets too close.

Behaviour without the right body signals

This is a really effective way to spot false emotions. If someone sounds friendly, look at their eyes to see if their eyes are friendly too. The tell-tale signs of anger rising up in another person can be seen long before it explodes into angry behaviour. For example, if you are teaching and instructing, look out for individual students who are looking at you with tense bodies and an unsmiling, fixed stare. They may be about to throw something at you!

Emotions can be a powerful tool in learning. Recent research has shown that body changes and internal perception are closely linked. If we experience strong body changes (it doesn't matter what triggers them in the first place) we think we are experiencing strong emotions. This phenomenon can cause difficulty because we may attribute the strong emotion to the wrong cause.

Dutton and Aron (1975) carried out some research in Canada to demonstrate this effect, which I find delightful. This research is called 'some evidence for heightened sexual attraction under conditions of high anxiety'. They picked an attractive young woman to interview some young men aged between 18 and 35. The interview was a tourist questionnaire and quite unexciting. Two groups were compared. One group of men were interviewed on flat level ground and the others were interviewed on a very wobbly, high, suspension bridge. After the interview, the men were asked to describe how attracted they were to the interviewer. The men interviewed on safe ground had an unemotional response but the men on the suspension bridge had found the woman highly attractive. They had mistaken their bodily reactions caused by fear of height and danger for the bodily changes experienced when falling in love. This experiment goes a long way to explain holiday romances and wartime marriages!

Emotional responses in learning are part of the student-teacher bond. Becoming aware of our emotions and reaction to them is part of learning too.

⇨ **STOP AND REFLECT** ⇦

Can you use *surprise* to highlight important learning points?

Should you use *fear* to ensure good safe practice?

Is it morally right to use *disgust* to enforce personal hygiene practice?

Should a teacher use justifiable *anger* to enforce a change in behaviour?

What *joy* do you give to your students?

Do you feel empathy with the *sorrow* that learners experience when they fail?

I think one of the best pieces of advice I ever had was to:

TEACH MERRILY

DOMAINS OF KNOWLEDGE

Benjamin Bloom (1964) worked out a very useful list of characteristics for what has to be learned in any skill or subject. He called each type of knowledge a 'domain'. He identified three domains: cognitive, psychomotor and affective.

Cognitive domain

This type of knowledge is concerned with thinking and mental processes. Bloom divided this field of knowledge into a hierarchy which began with the simplest form:

- knowledge – simple facts, like the distance the earth is from the sun
- comprehension – understanding the significance of simple facts and linking basic facts together
- application – knowing how to apply facts to the practical situation

- analysis – knowledge gained from the ability to break the whole down into component parts
- synthesis – knowledge of how to assemble ideas and facts to create a complete final product
- evaluation – knowledge of how to assess and evaluate all the other knowledge described above.

Psychomotor domain

This domain covers functional and procedural knowledge – the sort of knowledge which covers how to do things. This can be mental knowledge too, as every skill has an underpinning of facts and general rules, but perception and motor skills are the essentials of this domain. Bloom did not give details of knowledge in this area but here is a general description of the field:

- reflex movements – only the older parts of the brain are concerned, but this knowledge is important when learning coping skills
- basic movements – this knowledge is the intelligent use of an individual's own body
- perceptual abilities – the knowledge of how a person's body movements relate to all other physical objects in the surrounding space
- physical abilities – a self-knowledge of the range and extent of the body's capabilities
- skilled movements – the combination of procedural knowledge, perception and bodily movements combined to make a skilled performance
- non-discursive movements – the body movements which illustrate and accompany verbal communications and expressions of an individual's emotions and personality.

The affective domain

This is the most important area for the understanding of emotions. If the cognitive domain is knowing 'that', and the psychomotor domain is knowing 'how', the affective domain is knowing what you 'ought' to do. Emotions are our response to experiences but our responses reflect our attitudes and our view of what 'ought' to happen. In teaching and training we have firm ideas of what a skilled practitioner ought to do, which stretch far beyond cognitive knowledge and skills. We expect learners to have the right 'attitude', to 'care' and to be 'responsible'.

To explain the hierarchy which Bloom and his co-workers suggested for the affective domain I have taken an example. Suppose a young person is beginning on a course of study in one of the caring professions. Let us look at the stages of learning in the affective domain:

- *Receiving or attending* – at this stage of learning the young students pay attention only to what is being said and carry out what they are told to do. There is no real commitment at this stage other than a willingness to attend.
- *Responding* – as the learners begin to learn more about the care of other people, they become emotionally committed to their work. They comply with and applaud the work and the tasks being undertaken.
- *Valuing* – at this stage the learners start to take sides and defend the work they are undertaking. Any parent of young students will recognize when their young start to argue strongly in favour of the work and the area in which they are studying.
- *Organization* – this stage of emotional involvement with the work is when the learners start to rationalize and judge their work by professional standards. They become knowledgeable, are able to discuss issues which may arise and weigh up the strengths and weaknesses of given examples.
- *Characterization* – this is the stage of professional development when the work is internalized and becomes a characteristic part of the individual personality. The learners have come to 'believe' in their work and the profession is now part of their own self-image and self-esteem.

ACTIVITY

Take an example from your own teaching or training and analyse one session according to Bloom's taxonomy. When you have sorted out which knowledge is cognitive, which psychomotor and which affective then you will have a much clearer idea of how to make your presentation. Strategies of learning will be discussed in Book 3 of this series.

INTRAPERSONAL SKILLS

Howard Gardner (1985), a Harvard University professor, has a useful theory about 'multiple intelligence'. One of his six named intelligences is being intelligent about oneself. Intrapersonal intelligence means being able to handle our own emotions, feelings, thinking and memory. Control of a healthy body also comes into this intelligence area.

If we have a clear and realistic understanding of our own strengths and capacities then we have more time to spend on problem-solving and decision-making. Honey and Mumford (1982) described different preferred learning styles (Activist, Reflector, Theorist and Pragmatist) and this helps us to understand our own cognitive style. Mature and well-balanced people should be able to use all styles of learning so that they can choose the most effective learning method for any particular learning task.

Nowadays students are often asked to evaluate their own performance and to improve their own learning effectiveness. The only way to do this is to be able to understand oneself and work to a planned scheme of self-development.

One new term used in the discussion of intrapersonal skills is: 'meta-cognition'. Brian Redhead, the broadcaster, said, 'Understanding is the one genuine human happiness'. Meta-cognition means understanding oneself. This is the theme of this series of books.

HUMANISTIC PSYCHOLOGY

In Western society great emphasis is placed on the importance of the individual. This demand for recognition of individual needs rather than group needs has led to the development of the humanistic approach to learning. Our education and training systems recognize each learner as a unique individual. The teacher becomes not the instructor or the authority on a subject but the facilitator of learning. The teacher and trainer become the catalyst for the student to discover how he or she prefers to learn and to study. It is a supportive approach to student learning.

The movement of humanistic or phenomenological psychology has had a great influence on American and British life in the 1960s, 70s and 80s. Although several other psychologists have been part of the movement, the work of Maslow (1970) and particularly Carl Rogers (1970) has had the most influence. Here is a quote from the latter:

Ultimate value is placed on the dignity of the person.

Because experience is of primary importance for the student, humanistic psychologists have to use techniques in research which acknowledge the participants as joint experimenters rather than as subjects. Because the principle of meaningfulness to the individual is more important than objectivity, there has been some criticism of such research methods.

Rogers's work has been the basis of social changes in individual rights and individual demands. For example, the feminist and gay-liberation movements have drawn heavily on the importance placed on the right of individuals to achieve self-actualization. Business, the law, the health professions as well as education have moved towards the 'client-centred' approach which is recommended by Carl Rogers.

This approach has not been introduced without opposition. Some people are worried about the concentration on the rights of an individual rather than an individual's responsibility to society. The humanistic approach has been called a psychological 'sanction for selfishness'.

⇨ **STOP AND REFLECT** ⇦

Do you think that a theory which is suited to American society (both Maslow and Rogers are American) might be unsuitable for other societies?

Do students have the right to engage in the headlong pursuit of their own self-fulfilment?

Do all minority groups have an undisputed right to impose their self-fulfilment on the rest of society?

STUDENT-CENTRED LEARNING

One of the most obvious results of the acceptance of humanistic psychological principles is the current trend towards student-centred learning. Carl Rogers said that the teacher must facilitate the development of the individual's self-concept and help the individual student to achieve self-actualization. In order to achieve this both the teacher and the student must strive to be self-aware. Rogers felt that everyone has a self-image which might or might not be a true picture. Everybody has a vision of an ideal self – what they would really like to be. When the self-image and the ideal self are close together then the person is well-adjusted, able to be effective in learning and cheerful in their approach to life; if the self-image and ideal self are far apart, the gap produces discontent, ineffective learning and slow progress.

The idea of 'significant learning' is probably the most widely accepted of all Carl Rogers' theory. Students who have a realistic view of themselves will tackle learning tasks which are within, but just stretching, the frontiers of their knowledge and understanding. This effective and productive work is called 'significant learning' and, according to Rogers, students can achieve such learning if they are self-aware.

The teacher can help students to improve self-image by having:

- *empathy* with the students, ie, sharing a fellow feeling

- *congruence* with the students' ideals, ideas and ambitions, rather like sharing the same values and ambitions
- *positive regard* for the students – liking the students and being prepared to think the best of their efforts, work and opinions.

To implement this student-centred approach the teacher adopts strategies and tactics in the learning situation which include:

- encouraging students to participate and contribute to learning
- incorporating students' views into learning plans and schemes of work
- valuing the students' contribution
- using techniques which encourage full student participation
- encouraging peer group assessment and self-assessment.

⇨   **STOP AND REFLECT**   ⇦

Do you think that your students are fundamentally good people who will naturally pick out what is best for themselves and other people?

Do you think that students have enough basic understanding of your subject area to be able to decide for themselves the most effective way of learning?

Chapter 8

Stress and Anxiety

STRESS

I can remember arriving breathless and anxious in front of a large class on at least three occasions. Every time the subject of my lecture was to be 'Stress and anxiety'. My students did not believe me when I told them I lost my notes minutes before I was due to give the lecture; they laughed politely. But it was true – I had lost my notes and I was in a panic.

This says a great deal about the nature of stress. Most but not all stress is self-inflicted. In one study the stress levels of different experiences in life were rated according to the severity of stress resulting from the event. On this scale the death of a partner was rated as 100 points, divorce as 73 and marriage as 50. All sorts of life events involving occupational, financial, social and family changes were included. Everyone was asked to add up points for their previous year's experience so that an overall total could be produced. Their life stress was then estimated. Scores below 100 indicated a stress-free existence and those who scored over 200 were advised not to take long-term decisions at that time as their judgement could well be clouded by major stress.

'You are not suffering from depression; your life is depressing' – this is a reasonable suggestion when we are feeling down. The same is true of stress and anxiety.

STOP AND REFLECT

Ask yourself the question:

Is my life so stressful that I have good reason to feel that I am under stress?

Now try the question:

Am I really in danger so that I have a good reason for feeling anxious and afraid?

Hans Seyle (1974) worked on the problem of stress and the effect on individual performance. He described stress as the: 'Non-specific response of the body to any demand which was made upon it'.

The effects are much more far-reaching than might be thought possible.

ACTIVITY

As you read through the lists of non-specific bodily responses for the six different effects (Seyle, *Stress Without Distress*) note which responses your own body has when you feel stressed.

Subjective effects

Anxiety
Apathy
Depression
Frustration
Irritability
Shame
Low self-esteem
Nervousness
Aggression
Boredom
Fatigue
Guilt
Bad temper
Moodiness
Threat and tension
Loneliness

Behavioural effects

Being accident prone
Emotional outbursts
Loss of appetite
Excitability
Impulsive behaviour
Nervous laughter
Trembling
Drug taking
Excessive eating
Excessive drinking
Excessive smoking
Impaired speech
Restlessness

Cognitive effects

Inability to make decisions
Frequent forgetfulness
Mental blocks
Inability to concentrate
Hypersensitivity to
criticism

Physiological effects

Increased blood and
urine hormones
Increased heart rate and
blood pressure
Dilation of pupils
Hot and cold spells
Numbness and tingling
in parts of the limbs
Increased blood glucose
levels
Dryness of mouth
Sweating
Difficulty breathing
'Lump in the throat'

Health effects

Asthma
Chest and back pains
Diarrhoea
Dizziness
Frequent urination
Migraine
Nightmares
Amenorrhoea
Coronary heart disease
Feeling faint
Dyspepsia
Headaches
Neuroses
Insomnia

Psychoses	Psychosomatic disorders
Diabetes mellitus	Skin rash
Ulcers	Loss of sexual interest
Weakness	

Organizational effects

Absenteeism	Poor industrial relations
Poor productivity	High accident and labour turnover rates
Poor organizational climate	Antagonism at work
	Job dissatisfaction

But is stress necessarily a 'bad thing'?

In the film 'The Third Man', Harry Lime compared the creativity of Italy and Switzerland. He said that the stressful and turbulent history of Italy produced the magnificent art of Leonardo da Vinci and, after 300 years of peace, all that Switzerland had produced was the cuckoo clock. This relationship between the level of arousal and the level of performance is shown in Figure 8.1.

The performance of most people is generally most effective when they have a balance between low levels of arousal and over-excitement, but individuals differ in the amount of excitement required to reach this effectiveness. Some people like it 'hot' before they are really effective but other people thrive better in a calmer atmosphere.

Health audits and measurements of occupational stress indicators are big business nowadays; industry is beginning to count the cost of stress at work. In one study of shop floor workers it was shown that counselling could reduce sickness absence by two-thirds. How does stress affect teachers and students?

LEARNING AND ANXIETY

Life-chances and opportunities may depend on young children passing tests at school or adults gaining occupational qualifications; how might stress affect performance?

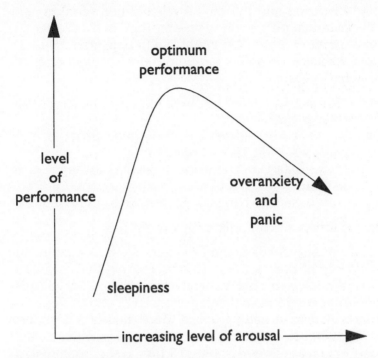

Figure 8.1 *Optimum performance*

Cognitive impairment

Eventually stress ceases to be a stimulant and begins to impair the ability to concentrate and organize thoughts logically. Learners are especially prone to worry about examinations; this is referred to as 'Test anxiety'. Students start to worry about failure and about their own inadequacies. These negative thoughts distract their attention and in an examination this might cause a failure to read and understand the test instructions. Failure to answer the correct number of questions or to cover all parts of a particular question are two of the quickest ways to fail an exam. Another effect of distraction may be the inability to remember facts which are normally easily recalled.

Contrastingly, people like me are happy to sit examinations and escape the monotony and boredom of continuous assessment or portfolio preparation. I find that one hasty revision and the careful organization of my time in the examination usually does the trick and involves the minumum of effort. You might like to note your responses to the statements below to find out if you are an examination person or not.

- If you are facilitated by the tension of an examination you might say:
  - I always work effectively when under pressure, especially when the task is important.
  - Once I start an examination I seem to forget to be nervous.
  - Nervousness when taking a test seems to make me do better.
  - Once I start on a task, nothing seems to distract me.
- If you are debilitated by the tension of an examination you might say:
  - While taking a test or examination, nervousness hinders me from doing well.
  - My fear of getting a bad grade makes me perform badly in a test or examination.
  - When I am poorly prepared for a test or examination, I get upset and do less well than even my restricted knowledge will allow.
  - The more important the test, the worse I do.
  - I always seem to remember the answers when I leave the examination room.

Emotional responses

There are three main emotional responses to stressful situations:

- anxiety – this is a reasonable reaction to a frightening or dangerous situation
- anger and frustration – this reaction may impair the ability to cope
- apathy and helplessness – this listlessness is even more debilitating.

Attitude of mind will affect an individual's reactions; with anxiety the emotional response may be much greater than the actual danger merits. This is called 'neurotic anxiety' and the individual may find it difficult to cope with stressful situations without help from other people.

Anger and frustration can be considered justifiable in some situations. These emotions often result in strong motivation so there may be occasions when a feeling of 'righteous indignation' acts as a spur to effective action.

Listlessness may be a reaction to stress which is learnt in early childhood. It may be a human reaction called 'learned helplessness' which is not fully understood. This attitude can be extremely harmful to any learning process. So, when can we be expected to cope for ourselves and when do circumstances make it very difficult for us to learn how to deal with stress without the help of other people?

COPING STRATEGIES

It is possible to learn strategies which can be used when facing a stressful situation; these are called coping strategies. However, as we have just noted, we have to recognize when we can learn to cope and when the situation is such that we need help from other people. We can't always be expected to cope on our own.

Sources of stress

- Traumatic events – situations outside the range of normal human experience; for example, earthquakes, wars, crashes and assaults such as rape.
- Life changes – birth, death, marriage, divorce, work, social, family and financial changes.
- Daily hassle – losing things, getting into debt, arguments, interruptions, minor illnesses.

Driving a car is a good example of 'daily hassle' which many of us experience, when we run a continuous risk of coming up against life-threatening situations. Skills required to cope with traumatic events in life can be learnt, even though they are usually specialized. When my husband was a young man he enjoyed motor racing and achieved quite a high standard. I have seen him use the specialist skills which he had acquired on racing circuits in emergency situations on the road. On more than one occasion he avoided a serious accident by using these specialist coping skills.

When there are many changes in life and the stress level is already high then specialist help is necessary to overcome additional stressful situations. It is in the area of daily hassle that we have the best chance of helping ourselves by learning to cope. This is why it is so worthwhile for the learners to get themselves well organized. When the learner can cope with study skills such as time management, the organization of notes, reading and writing skills and keeping fit, these skills can be transferred over to the learner's everyday life. The specialist study skills may be a helpful way to learn wider life skills.

PHYSICAL FITNESS

The traditional aim of education – 'A healthy body and a healthy mind' – is still a reasonable objective. While the human mind can function successfully in spite of pain, discomfort and physical deterioration, a healthy body functioning normally provides a much better basis for easier and more successful learning.

In certain areas of learning, it is important to ask whether the learner is physically capable of carrying out the task. This question is not asked of a student's mental capabilities because the normal human brain is capable of so much that it is most unlikely that the limits will be reached in a normal teaching situation, but a learner's physical capabilities are much more limited. There are some physical skills that many students will never acquire as they lack the bodily capability to carry out the motor movements.

When I was on a year's exchange in Australia, I spent a weekend in a remote forested area. My colleagues were splitting large logs for the wood-burning stove with a patent axe fitted with flying flanges which made spectacular splits once contact had been made. This was quite a jolly activity for a winter's morning and a crowd of us were eager to learn the skill. The axe was effective but very heavy. I was the only woman in the group who had enough strength to raise the axe over my head so that I could split the big logs. It gave me a great sensation of power and physical ability.

Log-splitting is a skill for which there is not much demand these days and so none of the other women were disturbed when they found that they couldn't use the axe. However, the lack of physical ability necessary for a skill which is in demand or is essential to fulfil a learner's ambition is much more serious. Those who wish to qualify as a dental technician, for example, must first pass a test of manual dexterity.

Students should decide whether it is worth the effort to learn coping skills to overcome their physical limitations. This could be a misplaced drive for self-esteem and similar effort in another field of learning might be more productive and less stressful. The trainer or teacher would be justified in offering advice, but should never attempt to make the ultimate decision for the individual learner.

TEACHER STRESS

Taking responsibility for other people's learning seems to be a threat to a teacher's health, or even life, these days:

- changes in curricula seem to be never-ending at present
- new skills are demanded of trainers and teachers
- the rights of the individual learner are emphasized but not the rights of the trainer or teacher
- teachers and trainers are held publicly responsible for motivating learners and ensuring their success.

These and other stresses are causing many teachers to take early retirement or risk a lessened life expectancy.

Training and educational managers could do a lot to relieve the teacher's current levels of stress by accepting the following suggestions:

- do not bully
- encourage a team approach

- do not expect 'super teacher' every time
- let staff know what is expected of them
- communicate in a rewarding and positive way
- establish a low-conflict climate
- use problem-solving models to resolve issues
- support teachers in their attempts to meet objectives
- place a higher value on subordinates.

The value our society places on the professions goes in cycles. For many years the teaching profession was highly respected; sadly, this is not so today. I remember when, under the early influence of the 1944 Education Act, the opportunity to stay on at school and go to university was regarded as a privilege. Teachers and lecturers, by virtue of their learning and expertise, commanded respect. Today education at all levels is regarded as a right and teachers and trainers can no longer expect respect. These changes have increased stress and anxiety and account for the low levels of morale within education and training.

STRESS MANAGEMENT IN LEARNING

There have been some fascinating developments in the control of physiological reactions to stress recently. It had been thought that there could be no voluntary control over the autonomic nervous system and the immune system. Now it is clear that conscious changes in the body's state can be made. One mechanism is bio-feedback. For example, it is possible to use a sound signal as a warning. At this stage a conscious and deliberate routine of relaxation can prevent the early stages of stress damage. The sound signal is switched off and normal muscular and bodily functions resumed. This method has also been successful in reducing high blood pressure and avoiding headaches.

ACTIVITY

Check the list of skills which help to control stress and improve learning to make sure that you follow the

advice that you ought to be giving to your own learners.
These skills include:

- breathing and posture
- relaxation
- meditation
- time management
- the ability to take time out and relax
- study skill management
- the ability to concentrate on deep study
- fitness and control of body weight
- a healthy diet and eating habits
- good sleep patterns
- an organized, well-balanced life style
- effective thinking habits
- a clear understanding of oneself.

Chapter 9

Learning Styles

'HOW DO I LEARN?'

The Further Education Unit is a research group of vocational teachers who are given leave from teaching to work on practical teaching and training problems. Some years ago the FEU produced a booklet called *How Do I Learn?* (1973). This question is, of course, almost impossible to answer but the team who wrote the booklet recommended an excellent way to start, by sorting out what has to be learnt, into:

M – what the learner must **m**emorize
U – what the learner must **u**nderstand
D – what the learner must be able to **d**o.

'MUD' sorting acts as a guide for a learning session to suit individual students who have their own preferred styles of learning.

<hr>

ACTIVITY

Using the MUD system.
Take any lesson or session plan and list the things that the learner has to do as M or U or D.

<hr>

This chapter will tackle the problem of matching individual learner styles to the general task of learning to memorize, understand and carry out skilled performances. The teacher or trainer cannot plan for the subject matter alone; he or she has to make certain that the subject material connects with the individual's own learning skills.

LEARNING 'BY HEART'

Learning 'by heart' or 'parrot fashion' was once the only form of learning in schools. After school many children went into a seven-year apprenticeship and all the apprentices learnt their trades by heart. The movements within a skill were practised over and over again until they become nearly automatic. Ask old ex-services personnel how they learnt in their careers in the armed forces and they will reply that they 'learnt by numbers', responding to shouted commands such as '1 – 2 – 3 – 1 – 2...' by carrying out movements they had learnt by heart. How fascinating to observe that my 6-year-old grandsons are both learning their multiplication tables 'by heart'.

I have never found spelling easy to master. During my school career rote learning (learning by heart) was regarded as a worthless activity. How I wish that it had not been so despised by my teachers! Rote learning of the rules of spelling might have saved me a great deal of teasing and embarrassment. Making me write words out a hundred times did nothing to help except giving me the satisfaction of inventing a multiple writing pencil. What I needed was to learn by heart the simple rules of spelling. Some skills are so important as a prerequisite for more complicated learning that the sooner and more certainly they are mastered the better for the individual learner. It is in these areas that rote learning comes into its own.

The first book of the series discussed the theory of learning; there are lots of different aids to memory which can be used and each learner should be encouraged to find a method which suits his or her own thinking and cognitive style. Age and previous memorizing experience, as well as personality, have an effect.

Age

I noted in Chapter 5 that young people memorize more easily than older people; mental flexibility, which is so useful in memorizing, does fall off with age, and the over 25-year-olds seem to have more difficulty than the under 25s.

The older learners in my class on navigation have difficulty in memorizing the International Regulations for the Prevention of Collision at Sea. A few who have kept up memorizing techniques find the task relatively easy but the majority find the task very daunting. This difficulty is usually overcome by using a multi-mode learning technique: if the students read the regulations aloud, rote learning is made easier; if they pre-record the regulations on a tape and play the tape while they read aloud they have three simultaneous inputs of the regulations and this method is even more effective. I wish I could make the International Regulations for the Prevention of Collision at Sea *smell* and then learning would be even easier!

⇨ STOP AND REFLECT ⇦

Do you think that age cramps your learning style or do you think, as President Roosevelt said, 'The only thing we have to fear is fear itself'?

> What can you do to reassure older learners that they can learn new skills?

Previous learning experience

Some people have a good 'inner eye' to learn by visualizing, sometimes called a 'photographic memory', and can improve their memory skills by practising their natural strength; others continuously practice some mental skills, like adding up sums of money, so that older market traders and bookmakers can rely on their ability to handle facts and numbers.

These skills for memorizing can be learnt and kept in constant practice. A friend went to a Quaker school where she learnt a section of text or poetry every day; the habit of daily rote learning remains with her to this day.

Personality

People with an eye for detail often seem to have good visual memory. Part of their personality seems to be the pleasure they gain from accuracy and order; tidy people make good memorizers.

Some people learn to memorize more quickly than others; most psychologists who try to define personality in terms of types and traits include intelligence or mental quickness as a factor in personal makeup and people who are described as 'quick' or 'bright' do seem to remember more easily and accurately than others. The obvious observation that some students are more intelligent than others sometimes clashes with any intention to treat all students equally. (The personality traits of intelligence and creativity are discussed in Chapter 10.)

LEARNING TO UNDERSTAND

Some years ago I had the strange feeling that I could look round a class of students and see a large question mark over the heads of those who could not understand what I was saying. It becomes easy with experience to recognize the signs: some have the relaxed, almost smooth, facial expression of having 'got it' but others have a contorted expression of doubt and uncertainty when they have failed to grasp some vital point. When learners have not understood the first explanation, repetition is the last thing they need. It is like shouting at a German speaker when he or she fails to understand English; only a totally different type of explanation will bring insight to those who failed on the first attempt.

When I find that a student has failed to understand I revert to a topic that he or she knows and cares about; using the topic as my starting point, I can launch into a second explanation. The technique is borrowed from Edward de Bono's ideas on lateral thinking which I first read about in his book *The Mechanism of Mind* (1969). The idea of lateral thinking is to encourage the thinker to take sideways, intuitive steps and break away from traditional logical lines of thought. Edward de Bono says that it helps the learner approach a problem from a new angle. When I try to give a second explanation from the learner's own interest I also use the well-tried principle of teaching from the 'known to the unknown'.

Teachers and trainers must never forget how difficult a problem seems before it is understood and how easy it seems once we do understand it. We all tend to have a reluctance to admit that we found anything difficult to learn! Some of the best teachers are those who had to struggle to learn because they know the methods they used to overcome their difficulties. I get impatient sometimes when my own students do not scamper after my train of thought as quickly and as easily as I imagine I learnt the topic.

Learning by understanding is a very individual process; some grasp explanations quickly, they 'think on their feet'; others need time and peace to think without distractions before they can accept something new. Like many people I often read something at night and wake up next morning full of bright ideas as if my brain were a personal computer which had been working away overnight.

LEARNING TO DO

How is a knack learnt? How does anyone learn a skill which can not be broken down into small separate movements? How do you learn to turn the painful, contorted hand and arm movements which occur when we pick up a violin for the first time into the gentle, controlled sway of the first violinist in a symphony orchestra?

Some people seem to be very quick to perceive when a body movement is right, feeling their way into the correct practical movements by using a general body-spatial intelligence. Certainly some people have musical abilities, such as perfect pitch, which makes musical learning much easier. Is this complex mixture of characteristics inherited or is it a general readiness to learn quickly? This question is discussed in the next chapter.

There is another training technique called 'Sitting by Nellie' which has been very much out of fashion lately; this is a method of learning to do something by watching what a skilled person does. Unfortunately Nellie is not often a trained trainer, so if you do not learn from her actions, she may find it hard to explain what she is doing. Still, for some people, watching and then trying to copy is all that is needed to learn quite complex skills.

LEARNING STYLES

Many training programmes demand that the trainers suit the learning methods to the individual learner and many teaching programmes demand that the students are kept interested and motivated in their studies. A typical training cycle is given in Figure 9.1. Catering for the individual is not easy in a large body of learners and even on a one-to-one basis the teacher has to identify an individual's preference.

This cycle of learning has been explained by Kolb in his 'experiential learning cycle' (1984) and the link between each stage of learning and personality has been developed by Honey and Mumford (1982) in their work on preferred learning styles.

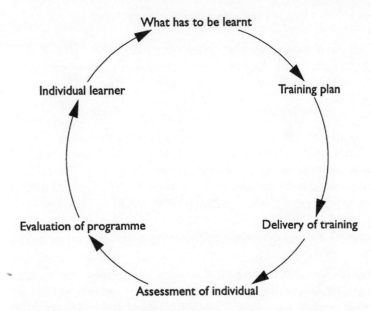

Figure 9.1 *A typical training cycle*

The cycle is a useful model because it represents the simple process of learning from experience and has wide application in traditional teaching. A simplified version is shown in Figure 9.2. Individual variations in learning and cognitive style are probably as varied as individual personalities but Kolb's cycle is a good place to start.

Because learning in this model is a continuous process which goes round and round, an explanation can begin at any stage but I shall start at the top where the learner has some active experience which could happen by chance, be an everyday occurrence, or it might be part of a simulation in a formal lesson. At this stage new information is fed into the working memory by the sense organs; it is an active stage.

Moving round to '3-o'clock' on the diagram, the learning process changes when the learner begins to think about what he or she has just experienced: this stage of pondering and reflecting on what has just occurred was the first topic of research into learning theory. Early psychologists studied the 'assimilation' and 'accommodation' of new

131

Appendix 4

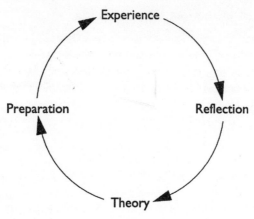

Figure 9.2 *A simplified version of Kolb's learning cycle*

knowledge and information, which is a more passive stage than active learning because the student starts to reflect on what has been learned. The stage of reflective observation is rather like an 'action replay' and so discussion, even if this discussion is within oneself, will help the learner to extract useful parts from activities and to assimilate the new experiences and understanding into existing learning.

The '6-o'clock' stage is called 'theory' and this is the stage at which the learner puts in other people's ideas and consults general rules. In teaching this is the stage of information-giving; in training it is the stage of coaching; and in self-instruction it is where the learner consults books, articles and other written and electronic references. It is where thinking about new information and comparing it with other theories takes place.

Moving on again to the '9-o'clock' position on the diagram, this is the stage where the learner starts to plan what to do next. The student has learnt something useful; he or she has reflected upon it and fitted the new learning into existing theory and so it is time to move on to another experiment with a new active learning experience. This is the practical planning or pragmatic stage.

The work of Honey and Mumford

Kolb's learning cycle has formed the basis of practical work in experiential learning and competency-based courses. Honey and Mumford (1982) used this cycle to produce a useful model of learning styles by linking the stages of Kolb's cycle to four descriptions of imaginary people who are happiest to work at each stage of learning (see Figure 9.3).

Appendix 4

Stage in Kolb's cycle   Honey and Mumford's name

Stage in Kolb's cycle	Honey and Mumford's name
Experience	Activist (active learning)
Reflection	Reflector (assimilation)
Theory	Theorist (working memory)
Preparation	Pragmatist (action planning)

Figure 9.3 *Comparison between Kolb's stages and learning style*

Honey and Mumford have produced a questionnaire with 20 questions aimed at each of the four learning preferences so that students can find their 'preferred learning style'; this quesionnaire is very popular with young students who sometimes use the results to explain why they did poorly at school! Many young people come out strongly as 'activists' and there are usually some 'pragmatists', but very few 'reflectors' or 'theorists'. Most intelligent adult learners come out very evenly-balanced between the four styles and this seems to point to a general observation that effective learners can use all four approaches. Appreciating the difference between the learning styles is important for younger learners because it allows the teacher to select a teaching method which is geared to the preferred learning style of the majority of the learning group. For example, I have found that effective learning results if I use lots of jolly activity for young trainees, a calm reflective approach for older learners, some tough theory for groups of young PhDs and a problem-solving approach for groups of managers and business students. Here are some extracts from the descriptions which Honey and Mumford use, together with some brief notes on the type of activities which will help learning in each of the preferred learning styles.

Active learners

Activists are described as people 'who welcome new experiences', 'enjoy things as they happen and greet every new sensation with enthusiasm'. They rush into every new experience 'without looking for drawbacks' and 'tend to take centre stage'. They are easily bored and prefer to be where the action is taking place: they are happy to combine with other people and treat any difficulty as an opportunity for problem-solving. It is no wonder that a lot of young people are delighted by this refreshing description.

At present, the process of active learning is very much in fashion for both teaching and training because the active learner is perceived as one who is motivated and interested. Lecturers and instructors are encouraged to make sure that there are lots of things for students to do. These ideas fit in with Carl Rogers' (1970) approach for student-centred learning (discussed in Chapter 7) and again it is a deliberate attempt to try to meet the individual's particular needs. I am not so certain that active learning meets all the needs of effective learning but it certainly gets the learner off to a good and enthusiastic start. My reservation is that I wonder if, with all this activity going on, the learner has the time to 'engage brain'.

The person who likes active learning will enjoy learning through games, competitive teamwork tasks and role play.

Reflective learners

The Honey and Mumford 'reflector' is a person who has a cautious, thoughtful and low-profile image, preferring to watch other people and taking the back seat as a listener. They are calm, take their time and prefer to act only after all the available information has been collected; they like to look at every problem from all available viewpoints. What is described seems to be the behaviour of a slightly older person – don't we learn to become more reflective and a little more cautious with age?

This stage is clearly a process of the assimilation of knowledge. More advanced personality theory is covered in the next stage of this series of books, but it is useful to look here at the work of George Kelly (1955) on what happens in reflection. Kelly regarded all people as having a set of personal templates or standards against which they measure each new experience; when the new information fits our existing system we just confirm what we thought already, but when something doesn't fit into our measuring standards then we have to think about the new thing and either reject it or alter our template system to accommodate the new knowledge.

Reflection is also important when you are trying to put together evidence of prior experience and knowledge; learners can gain access to many programmes by producing evidence for APL (Accreditation of Prior Learning) or APEL (Accreditation of Prior Experiential Learning) with the presentation of a portfolio of evidence of what you have learned before. It is not enough to say that, 'I did this...', 'I went to...', 'I attended ...'.

To gain credit for having covered course material or being competent in particular areas you have to reflect upon your experiences and what you have seen and done so that you show that you have learned; the secret of good evidence for APL and APEL is to be able to write down your reflections on your learning.

The person who likes to learn in this reflective manner prefers learning activities which are observational, like viewing video, or self-directed, like carrying out an investigation.

Theorists

Honey and Mumford describe the theorist as someone who learns by investigating the evidence according to general rules, carrying out study in logical steps. They will use all the stages of cognitive knowledge described in Bloom's theory of the cognitive domain (see Chapter 1). These learning types like to stick to step-by-step processes and are not happy with intuitive leaps; to the young activists, these people would be 'eggheads'.

Most people do not think in logical steps, so this type of approach has to be learned and logic is difficult to handle until you have learned the rules and steps. This stage of Kolb's cycle is the process of working with concepts. It is the area of thinking in rules and general applications, when the learner puts forward hypothetical ideas which have to be tested.

Thinking in abstract terms is an important stage of learning development; without it the learner cannot use the handy short-cuts of symbols and general principles and learning becomes a very slow and roundabout process. Here is an example: to understand the reaction –

$$HCl + NaOH \rightarrow NaCl + H_2O$$

you have to know about and be able to think in terms of chemical formulae and the general concepts of chemical reactions. It takes much longer to say:

> If you take a dilute solution of hydrochloric acid and mix it with a dilute solution of an alkaline substance called sodium hydroxide, these two chemicals will interact to form common salt which is called sodium hydroxide, and water will be the by-product.

In my example it takes four lines of English prose to describe the simplest possible chemical reaction: imagine how many words it would take to describe a large molecule like a protein, with hundreds of linked elements and a variety of important structural details. The use of chemical symbols and structural diagrams makes chemistry understandable, when a word description would be impossible to grasp because of length and complexity.

Theorists think with symbols and general rules which make for effective and accurate learning; they prefer learning activities which methodically explore the interrelationship between ideas, principles and examples of general applications.

Pragmatists

Honey and Mumford describe pragmatists as people who are happy to learn by trying out ideas in practice. They are the people who want to get on with the job, responding to a challenging demand with an enthusiastic plan of action; they are not concerned with general principles because their only criterion is, 'Does it work?'

Pragmatism is associated in education with the work of John Dewey (1952), who experimented with a pragmatic approach to learning in his school in Chicago at the end of the nineteenth century; he was still writing about progressive learning methods in the early 1950s. The pragmatic approach always has a practical theme: the learner works on real-life problems and learns from those who have solved the problems already. The 'if it works, it's good' approach to learning is the basis of a more democratic approach to teaching, and Dewey's ideas have been very influential in education for many years. However, there is an important proviso: if you start from a sound basis of good practice, the student will learn to develop further sound practice, but if you start from a basis of poor practice and unsound principles, then the learner perpetuates poor practice.

In the current UK National Vocational Qualifications scheme, a representative committee, known as a 'lead body', for each occupational area is responsible for setting the national standards for the industry. The quality assurance system to guarantee that these standards are maintained is operated by assessors who have current qualifications within the industry. This system has the great benefit of being designed to make sure that new recruits to an industry are given training which is relevant to current industrial demands. When industrial standards are high, the national standards set by an industrial lead body are sound and based on good practice, and there is good local quality assurance control, then all new learners will be trained to high skills level. However, this is not always the case. I have seen trainee cabinet-makers being taught how to make dovetailed joints in wooden furniture where the two sections slide in and out with a firm and completely matched smoothness which comes from superb craft skills, but also I have seen trainees shown how to gouge out the underside of a 'dovetail' so that it matches 'alright' on the surface but is hollowed out underneath; unfortunately, bad furniture joints are quicker to make than getting a solid fit. If the principle of pragmatism is the only thing guiding learning, then national standards of learning are set at current practice which may be unacceptably low.

The 'pragmatist' prefers to learn in a down-to-earth way with learning activities which are as close as possible to real working situations; they are people who thrive on learning with computer simulations of real experiences and from direct work experience.

The flexible learner

Although it is always useful to break down a system into parts so that you can understand each bit before attempting to understand the whole, the disadvantage is that an integrated understanding of the 'whole' may be lost. While it may help young learners to identify with active learning so that they are motivated to learn, eventually they will have to learn to use all styles of learning because this is the route to becoming a mature and independent learner. Kolb's learning cycle summarizes the progression and the skilled learner can enter at any stage, repeating the sequence over and over again.

I think that it is selling young learners short to pretend that all they want to learn can be achieved in a style which they find easy, because some worthwhile learning is not facile. The basic skills of numeracy, literacy, memorizing, thinking and being able to handle rules and concepts are learnt by being able to operate as an activist, a reflector, a theorist *and* a pragmatist. If a young learner fails to achieve these basic learning skills then most advanced study becomes impossible or, at least, very difficult indeed. Some youngsters should be dragged screaming backwards if necessary into basic skills so that the rest of their lives are not permanently blighted.

LATERAL THINKING

Edward de Bono (1969) has made a most useful contribution to learning theory. His whole concept of lateral thinking encourages:

- learning thinking skills
- creative problem-solving
- the generation of original ideas.

When he talks about individual talents or natural abilities he uses the example of different levels of skills in driving a car; just as some people are skilled drivers, so some people are skilled thinkers. The analogy continues with the comparison between a good driver who can do very well in a small car, and a bad driver who may not be very successful in a high performance classic car; in just the same way a good thinker operates his or her modest inherited talents as a very successful learner, whereas a poor thinker can ruin great inherited mental talent!

Chapter 10

Intelligence and Creativity

CONCEPTS

Wisdom
Achievement
Intelligent behaviour
Talent
Intelligence
Concept formation
Learning mental skills
Creativity
Learning to be creative

WISDOM

Nobody in education and training talks much about wisdom. Many of us will utter such platitudes as: 'The day I stop learning is the day I turn my toes up', 'You are never too old to learn', or 'Learning is a life-long objective', but what is our ultimate objective? I think it may be the pursuit of wisdom or, if you like, the creation of a wise human being.

What is wisdom? It certainly isn't something that you are born with because wisdom seems to be something that you acquire as you go along. What may wisdom be? When a person chooses to try to achieve wisdom, there are three things which have to be learnt: knowledge, practice and judgement:

- You have to know a lot in order to be wise and so there is a definite knowledge base which has to be learnt and stored in your long-term memory.
- There is a practical basis to wisdom because you have to know how things happen or how to do things; this means that wisdom has a procedural, practical side which comes from experience of many different methods of tackling problems and approaching new situations.
- Judgement comes into an analysis of wisdom – making a wise choice and deciding between several alternatives. The proof of the wise decision is success, by which I mean a result which satisfies all aims and objectives.

ACHIEVEMENT

Teachers and trainers looked again at individual achievement in the 1950s when Carl Rogers introduced 'student-centred learning'; he had a great influence on changing the approach to learning. At the same time, Robert Glaser proposed a 'mastery learning approach' linked to criterion-referenced testing and competency-based learning; both writers raised questions about traditional education.

Glaser, followed by W James Popham (1978), highlighted the difference between the traditional testing of learning and criterion-referenced testing.

- in *traditional testing*, each individual is measured mainly against other people learning the same thing at the same time
- in *criterion-referenced testing*, each individual is measured against a set of agreed standards, independent of other learners.

There are strengths and weaknesses in the trend towards using achievement as a measure of learning. On the plus side, learners have a very clear picture of what they are able to do, so that this positive strength is quickly incorporated in the learner's self-image and may well increase individual self-esteem and motivation. Such constructive reassurance is helpful to the individual's pursuit of wisdom.

The other side of this is that the achievement of set standards means that the individual does not operate outside the bounds of other people's idea of competence; there is little room for creativity and originality. This limitation has additional problems in decision-making and judgement: if the choice of alternatives is restricted to a limited knowledge base then the individual may never gain access to greater fields of choice.

Competency-based learning can restrict individual people to a slow rate of learning because personal achievement and progress are limited to the pace set by the trainers, teachers, assessors, examiners and the 'gurus' of validating bodies. Conventional examination systems are almost as pedantic and I think that too much time is wasted in needless assessment of achievement and the sitting of examinations. There is a danger of the learner being bored to death by assessment.

INTELLIGENT BEHAVIOUR

Howard Gardner (1985), Professor of Psychology at Harvard University, puts forward a very useful theory of multiple intelligences in which he suggests that there are many ways we can demonstrate intelligent behaviour; here are six examples.

Verbal intelligence

The traditional idea of intelligence requires that people have verbal expressional skills; they include grammar and literature skills, verbal expression and fluency (these competences of intelligence are described as language skills in Chapter 7 of the first book in the series). Verbal intelligence is a basic requirement of learning in almost every area; it is necessary for understanding the words so essential to thought and memory storage.

Mathematical intelligence

The next most popular idea of general intelligence is that people should be numerate; numeracy is the basis of learning and being competent in many subjects. A person who is not skilled in number-crunching can be at a disadvantage because mathematical ideas are the basis of much science and technology, research and occupational practice.

Spatial intelligence

The ability to use three-dimensional skills is essential in engineering, architecture and all design forms, and many creative arts and practical crafts. The perception of solid shape in a fluid medium is basic to so much human activity and also to so much mental understanding of basic principles that this intelligence is crucial for many occupations. I feel that this type of intelligence can be taught provided that it is addressed at an early age.

Bodily intelligence

This is where Professor Gardiner's theory starts to get really interesting, because he moves away from the traditional intelligences and claims that people can show intelligence with bodily movement, music and other areas of human talent. When I was reading his theory for the first time I experienced a sudden insight into his ideas through watching a man with a rope and a chainsaw cutting down a large tree outside my window. He started at the top, literally cutting away the platform upon which he stood. His body movements were delicately-controlled but strong and effective; the chainsaw whirred away as he swung about his task and when he finally lowered himself from the short main trunk to the ground, a fascinated crowd, like me, broke into spontaneous applause. It was a supreme example of bodily intelligence.

Interpersonal skills

There are many names for this sort of intelligence: 'social skills', 'communication skills' or even the ability to be 'street-wise'. Intelligent action when dealing with other people is essential for so many activities. A teacher can see even a genius lose understanding because he or she could not deal intelligently with the students. Universities are full of such people: some lecturers seem to take a perverse pride in being rotten communicators (though others remember how difficult some subjects seem when you are starting to study).

Intrapersonal skills

This is the skill of knowing yourself; without intelligent use of your own skills, no other learning is possible. When people work from an insecure, confused personal position it is like an inefficient engine – they spend too much time and talent on internal work and cannot manage to be effective outside. The key to personal effectiveness is intelligent use of one's own personal cognitive, psychomotor and affective skills.

When a teacher or trainer takes this broad view of intelligent behaviour, they have a good platform upon which to rest efforts to help students to learn. Effective learning can take place in all aspects of human activity provided that there are no artificial barriers to what is considered to be intelligent behaviour.

TALENT

Because each person is unique, all people are not equal and because all people are not equal, some people are born with more talents than others. This simple piece of logic has stuck in the gullets of many educationalists who have the laudable intention of wanting to provide equal opportunities for all. Later in the chapter I will look at questions of quality versus equality, but first I will look at individual freedom of expression.

Studies of personality show that an individual achieves the greatest happiness and self-fulfilment if he or she makes the most of inborn natural talent; the pursuit of excellence in the area of natural ability seems to be a good thing. The problem is that natural talent may be hidden and genius does not always make an early showing in childhood; for example, without an opportunity to hear music and get your hands on an instrument, musical talent may be stillborn.

Plenty of opportunity to try new things seems to be a good policy in early development but there are two more difficulties which stand in the way of the open development of talent. First, there is a cognitive element, as well as psychomotor and affective skills, in intelligent behaviour and wisdom. This means that academic and thinking skills are basic to all other learning and cannot be avoided however practical the task in hand; a bit of 'book learning' is essential for the successful achievement of all competences and skills. Second, the individual's creative talents are not fully developed unless some expression of this creativity is passed on to other people. Thus the creator not only has to be able to use cognitive skills but also to employ powers of interpersonal communication if the new ideas which come from their own creativity are to be passed into general human understanding. Fully developed talents cannot exist in a vacuum: some evidence of creativity has to be communicated to someone else.

INTELLIGENCE

Intelligence has had a 'bad press' in training and educational circles because of the use of intelligence tests to allocate education resources to children. Scorn is usually poured on the method of testing and the original research in the field; endless examples of bad decisions which arose from intelligence testing are quoted. People who criticize intelligence testing usually end with the 'cruncher' that the speaker or writer failed the tests as well!

Let us look at some well-established facts:

- Some people seem to be better at calculating simple mathematical problems inside their heads than others.
- Some people seem to be quicker at understanding written English than others.
- Some people seem to be better able to recall facts than others.
- Most people improve in simple, mental abilities with age until about 25 years when the flexibility of simple mental calculations seems to fall away unless these skills are practised constantly.
- If you have quick and accurate simple mental agility and recall, all other learning becomes easier.

I think that three conclusions can be drawn from these fairly universally accepted statements:

There are general mental skills which help with all learning.

Mental skills are best learned when young and kept in practice.

Some people have more mental skills than others.

⇨ **STOP AND REFLECT** ⇦

Intelligence tests are criticized for being too narrow when they concentrate on calculation and language but what else do we do in our working memory but use calculation and language?

The concept of intelligence is criticized for being culture specific. Do you think that the idea of intelligence is 'intelligent behaviour within a culture' and so has to be culture specific?

If these simple mental skills are part of what we call intelligent behaviour, then young children should not be allowed to choose ignorance from the techniques at school because the lack of the skills is too damaging for

---

later learning. This is one of those cases of a clash between principles where one advantage – the chance to grow to be independent – clearly outweighs the right of the individual to choose. Ignorance now will not assist independence later. Adult learners may have missed out in earlier years and have a hard battle to make up the deficit.

CONCEPT FORMATION

Another mental skill which appears to be necessary for a person to become fully mature and an autonomous human being is the ability to form and use concepts in thinking processes. Concepts are generalized ideas which can be translated into rules; the ability to apply rules to problem-solving is essential for all advanced learning, whatever the field of study.

The changeover from the simple, solid example-type of 'thinking' to the more complex 'conceptual thinking' takes place at about the age of puberty or a bit younger. Some children at school never make the swap and I believe that this failure condemns the growing person to a lifetime of limited thinking. Of course, the trainer and teacher can go on explaining in concrete terms and some progress can be made, but more advanced thoughts and complex theories simply cannot be understood unless the flexibility of formal thinking can be used.

LEARNING MENTAL SKILLS

Although the National Curriculum and new techniques for dealing with truancy at school may help future generations of learners, how are we to help *adult* learners to learn? We have just discussed concept formation, now try an activity on concept formation which you can use with your learners.

ACTIVITY

Concept formation as a mental skill.
Select a concept from your own teaching area and make an analysis of how you are going to give your learners the experience of thinking in a formal way. It will help you to formulate a good strategy if you go through the following list.

What is the concept you want to teach?

What principles have to be understood before the concept can be taught?

List the underlying principles in a sequence for presentation.

How will you check that the learners have understood the essential underpinning principles before you start on concept formation? Write short questions which will quickly indicate such understanding.

What are examples of the concept which your learners may have experienced before? If there are no personal examples of the concept, can you think of general cases which occur in everyday life?

Write a series of case examples of your concept which are from the learner's experience which can be set as learning tasks.

Write a series of questions suitable for discussion after the learner has tackled the core examples.

In Book 3 I will be looking at strategies for learning, but this activity will give some guidance as to how to put the theory of learners' needs into practice. Do not forget when you come to use the discussion questions that it is important to let the learner talk out loud to help learning and form associations within the memory.

CREATIVITY

Pure original genius is very rare indeed and I don't suppose that many of us can honestly say we have had the privilege of coming across it.

Creativity in training and education is confined to the ability to create new ideas, applications and solutions as a consequence of using skill and knowledge. Indeed the creativity 'test' in training is a measure of how far the learner has outstripped the teacher of the subject to become autonomous and independent. If the 'test' is 'passed', it is a credit to the trainer because it shows that the natural talents of the learner have been given full scope.

There is a tendency to say that Arts are different from the Sciences and to suggest that arts people are creative whereas scientists are merely intelligent, but I am opposed to this view. I think that all excellent practice depends on both creativity and intelligence.

LEARNING TO BE CREATIVE

Creativity can be expressed as knowing the rules and going beyond them. This definition is very helpful because a teacher or trainer can only set up the right conditions for a learner to be encouraged to be creative; the final step towards creativity has to come from the learner working alone.

Here is a list of characteristics which seem to be important to creativity:

curiosity
originality
independence
imagination
non-conformity
ability to see relationships
full of ideas
experimenter
flexibility
persistence

constructive
liking for complexity
day-dreamer.

These suggested characteristics may only be useful to the teacher as an indication of potential creativity. What the teacher or trainer needs to know is how to encourage creative behaviour. A great deal has been written on the topic but four factors seem to be commonly agreed as useful in encouraging creativity.

Fluency

This refers to an easy familiarity with all aspects of the subject or topic. The best example I have come across of a craftsman being fluent with every aspect of his trade was a shoemaker I saw in Australia. This master of his craft had a specialized understanding of hardened steel so that he could grind knives to the shape he required to cut the leather for his original shoe designs. Originality seems to be an unconscious part of the creative person and because the topic seems to be of such burning interest, every detail is eagerly sought, discussed and digested before it is stored away in the long-term or the procedural memory. Such enthusiasm and dedication make all problems of cognitive ability and powers of expression unimportant.

Flexibility

When I was studying nutrition, our professor decided that all nutrition theory was useless if the food produced was inedible, so we were all taught to cook. The lecturer was determined we should be fully familiar with our trade, so a massive kitchen was lined with every known make and type of cooker: each week we progressed round cookers in the circuit and by the end of the year we had all cooked on solid fuel, gas, bottled gas, paraffin, electric and woodburning stoves. This chance at flexible learning made some of us very creative cooks! The flexibility to work with every aspect of your trade seems an important part of creativity.

Originality

The new solution or creation must be novel, and not a direct copy of something already known. The novel object must be appropriate for its purpose; originality doesn't just mean being different. A new idea or creation should solve a problem or fit a function or form; in addition an original creation should have some completeness in form – a Gestalt wholeness.

It is difficult ever to say that something is truly original; I feel that some improvement in originality can be encouraged by teaching, but at the end of the day you are on your own.

Elaboration

One of the best ways to encourage creativity is to help learners to work out variations on a theme. This is rather like the musical variations which are used in jazz; by playing around with materials and ideas, the variations trigger new thoughts and solutions.

References

Adorno, T W (1947) *The Authoritarian Personality*, New York: Norton.

Argyle, Michael (1975) *Bodily Communication*, London: Methuen.

Argyle, Michael (1987) *The Psychology of Happiness*, London: Routledge.

Atkinson, Atkinson, Smith and Bem (1993), *Introduction to Psychology* (11th edn) London: Harcourt Brace Jovanovich.

Bales, R F (1950) *Interaction Process Analysis*, University of Chicago Press.

Berne, Eric (1968) *Games People Play*, Harmondsworth: Penguin.

Bloom, Benjamin S (1964) *The Taxonomy of Educational Objectives*, London: Longman.

Bruner, Jerome S (1960) *The Process of Education*, Boston: Harvard University Press.

de Bono, Edward (1969) *The Mechanism of Mind*, London: Jonathan Cape.

Dewey, John (1952) *Experience in Education*, Collier Macmillan.

Dutton and Aron (1975) 'Some evidence for heightened sexual attraction under conditions of high anxiety', *Journal of Personality and Social Psychology*, 57, 1082–90.

Eysenck, H J (1981) *Dimensions of Personality*, Oxford: Pergamon.

Fensterheim, Herbert (1976) *Don't Say YES When You Want To Say NO*, London: Futura.

Gardner, Howard (1985) *The Mind's New Science*, London: Harper Collins.

Gibbs, G (1973) *How do I Learn?*, London: FEU.

Guildford, J P (1954) *Psychometric Methods*, McGraw Hill.

Heron, John (1986) *Six-Category Intervention Analysis* (2nd edn) Human Potential Research Project, University of Surrey.

Honey P, and Mumford, A (1982) *The Manual of Learning Styles*, Maidenhead: Peter Honey.

Janis, Irving (1982) *Groupthink, Psychological Studies in Policy Decisions and Fiascos* (2nd edn), Boston: Houghton Mifflin.

Kelly, George (1955) *The Psychology of Personal Constructs*, New York: W W Norton.

Kolb, David A (1984) *Experiential Learning Experience as a Source of Learning and Development*, Englewood Cliffs, NJ: Prentice Hall.

Luft, Joseph (1970) 'Johari's Window', *Group Processes: An Introduction to Group Dynamics*. National Press Books.

Maslow, Abraham H (1970) *Motivation and Personality*, New York: Harper & Row.

Popham, W James (1978) *Criterion-Referenced Measurements*, Prentice Hall.

Rogers, C R (1970) *On Becoming a Person: A Therapist's View of Psychotherapy*, Boston: Houghton Mifflin.

Seyle, Hans (1974) *Stress Without Distress*, London: Hodder and Stoughton.

Steiner, George (1978) *Has Truth a Future?* BBC Publications.

Index